D0443011

A voice
in our
wilderness

A voice in our wilderness

John Husar's timeless writings on the outdoors, strange meals, and life's simple moments

TRIUMPH
B O O K S
CHICAGO

The royalties from this book will go to The John Husar Outdoor Education Endowment, created by the Illinois Conservation Foundation. The goals designated for the endowment are the creation of the John Husar Under Illinois Skies Endowment. The foundation will provide urban children with outdoor opportunities. The second goal is the creation of the John Husar Lookout Point at Mississipi Palisades State Park to remember his contributions to the outdoors.

Library of Congress Cataloging-in-Publication Data

Husar, John, 1937–2000
    A voice in our wilderness : John Husar's timeless writings on the outdoors, strange meals, and life's simple moments / John Husar
        p. cm.
    A collection of the author's Chicago tribune columns.
    ISBN 1-57243-614-X
    1. Outdoor recreation. 2. Hunting. 3. Fishing. 4. Husar, John, 1937–2000 I. Title.

GV191.6.H87 2004

2003071198

This book is available in quantity at special discounts for your group or organization.
For further information, contact:
Triumph Books
601 South LaSalle Street Suite 500
Chicago, Illinois 60605
(312) 939-3330
Fax (312) 663-3557

Printed in U.S.A.
ISBN 1-57243-614-X
Design by Laura Husar Garcia and Tony Majeri Jr.
Chapter photos by Laura Husar Garcia
Photo insert photos from Husar family collection

EDITORS' NOTE

Early on in this project, it became apparent that you could blindfold yourself, grab a bunch of John Husar columns at random and have enough material for a fabulous book. In that regard, editing *A Voice in Our Wilderness* was easy.

But then came the formidable task of winnowing down the hundreds of articles John wrote in his 15 years as the *Chicago Tribune's* outdoor editor. Each of us was forced to toss out some favorites, but we have plenty of fodder for *The Best of John Husar, Volume II.* Come to think of it, that's not a bad idea.

We are grateful to *Chicago Tribune* editor *Ann Marie Lipinski,* former *Tribune* operations editor *Dale Cohen* and *Tribune* deputy managing editor for operations *Randy Weissman* for their help and encouragement in shepherding this manuscript into print. *Tribune* researchers *Judy Marriott* and *David Turim* were invaluable as we compiled the early drafts of this book.

Bill Cullerton Sr., Bob Marshall, Chauncey Niziol and *Charlie Potter* generously shared memories of time spent in the field with John.

Most of all, we thank John's family—his wife, *Louise,* and his daughters, *Kathryn Coyle* and *Laura Husar Garcia.* They shared their time, their energies, their photographs and most of all their memories of our beloved colleague, the gentle giant of the woods.

Mike Conklin, Bob Condor and Kerry Luft

CONTENTS

THE GENTLE GIANT

John Husar, the *Chicago Tribune*'s beloved outdoor writer, was born on Chicago's South Side to Slovakian and Lithuanian parents.

He majored in journalism at the University of Kansas, where he played football and worked at first job at the school paper. From there, he worked for several newspapers before landing at the Tribune, where he would work for 34 years.

Early in his career, Husar worked on such breaking news stories as the Richard Speck murder investigation and the McCormick Place fire. But he mostly covered sports, especially golf and the Olympic Games.

In 1985 he became the paper's outdoor writer and became a pioneer in adding the issues of environment and ecology to the beat, accompanying traditional reporting on hunting and fishing.

A huge man who stood well over six feet tall, he wrote with a light touch and an artist's eye. His laugh could shake thunder from the clouds.

He was nominated for a Pulitzer Prize in 1980 for a series on the potential for conserving natural areas along the Des Plaines River.

Husar died of hepatitis C on July 20, 2000, aged 63, a little more than a week after he received part of a new liver from a live donor.

"No more gentle soul ever was in so large a man," wrote Tribune colleague Bernie Lincicome.

FOREWORD

Once upon a time, John Husar was my roommate. It was not a particularly happy time for me, because it was during the 1984 Winter Olympics. I was not then, nor am I now, a fan of either winter or the Olympics, and to make matters worse, that particular snowball fight took place in Sarajevo, Yugoslavia, a Godforsaken glacier if ever there was one.

Naturally, for three weeks, I counted the days until I could see Sarajevo in my rear-view mirror. Just as predictably, Big John loved every minute. Every day was Christmas Day for him, anyway, but when he arose each morning to find three or four or five more feet of the white stuff outside our apartment windows, Big John became deliriously happy. Before long, many of us curmudgeons in the media contingent referred to him, endearingly, as "Capt. Snow."

Understand that Big John could write about anything, anywhere, with clarity, brilliance and above all, zeal. He was a superior golf reporter at the Chicago Tribune, then moved on to a general column about mainstream sports—bats, balls, sticks, pucks. Big John was excellent, although he probably wasn't comfortable dealing with spoiled and pampered athletes who didn't quite share his perpetual joy about life. Big John's shiny disposition and deep, hearty laugh were misplaced in somber, serious major league locker rooms.

By someone's stroke of genius, Big John was then assigned the outdoor beat, and to say he embraced it is a colossal understatement. Again with fondness, we quipped that Big John had found his Shangri-La because he didn't have to interview flora or fauna. But, of course, it was more than that. Talk about a man who could take a blank canvas and paint magnificent pictures with words from the heart. His essays about woods and waters humbled those of us who typed away in climate-controlled press boxes, spewing scores and highlights.

Every day was an adventure for Big John, a challenge to his creative genius, and I doubt that he considered his work to be a job. It wasn't his duty to put his thoughts down on paper. It was his privilege.

I realized as much in Sarajevo, where I was only too happy to cover a hockey game while he burrowed through snowdrifts, bundled up from head to toe, to some exotic venue hours away to witness some obscure competition at a mountain or ski slope bearing a name that only he could pronounce or spell.

Then Big John would return to the apartment in the wee hours, exhausted and exhilarated. I had been to our shower without the curtain and was shivering in bed when he would call his wife, Louise, in Chicago, gushing about what he had observed that day and how they would have to return to Sarajevo in the near future on vacation. Often, I thought about telling Big John he was crazy. But, of course, he could have whipped me with one hand tied behind his back, blindfolded. Thank goodness he was a gentle giant.

Now, in retrospect, I realize Big John was bigger than all of us in many more important ways than size. In a business that demands a lot of production under tight deadlines, we tend to go from the gee whiz mode to aw, nuts. We become cynical and jaded, but Big John never, ever went there and did that. He cared dearly about every syllable he authored from every outpost. We joked with Big John about his temperament, but it was certainly not because we mocked him. On the contrary, deep down, we envied him.

You can't teach passion, and that's what separated Big John from the masses. Alas, as I look back at our brief experience in bonding at Sarajevo, I only wish I could have absorbed a few lessons Big John was imparting for free. Some of us exist, others truly live. I missed that point in the apartment we shared and now, I miss Big John.

How cruel it is that, of all people, John Husar's time was cut short. He really deserved be with us longer. His campfire was extinguished way too soon. But while we can rue the fact that was cheated by time, he left nothing on the table while he was here. How many of us, as we perform our daily chores, can honestly make that statement about ourselves?

−Bob Verdi

CHAPTER ONE
DAYBREAK

Oversleeping was not an option for John Husar. He didn't appreciate a late sleeper among fishing or hunting buddies, either. He simply didn't want to waste any part of any day, especially the morning's first light. Too much natural beauty that might be missed out there if you were a sleepyhead.

John savored new beginnings. Whether it was a brand-new day, first meetings or reviving an old haunt. He most cherished the many "firsts" he experienced his young grandchildren. It affirmed his strong feelings about the natural order of things.

May 29,1994

Kids learn from master and grandfather too

You might say I waited a lifetime for the moment. I certainly day-dreamed of little else for five whole years. I played the scenarios this way and that. Things had to be perfectly right when I took my grand-sons on their first real fishing trip.

Oh, they had been in a boat with me once before. We dunked min-nows for a few hurried minutes last fall in a corner of Aldo Marchetti's lake, and the older kid actually reeled in two crappie and a perch. He mostly wondered why those flopping fish were so "angry." He still was a little young.

But now he had been primed with his own spincast rod and practice plug, so he knew the sense of flinging a weight through air. Now it was a matter of the right phone call, which my good buddy Spence Petros made last week.

The editor of Fishing Facts magazine, a renowned angler and teacher, said he had found the mother lode of big bluegills on a little point beside an inlet at Bull Valley Hunt Club.

"If you want those kids to catch fish," he said, "that's where you'll want to go."

Spence came, too, making sure I didn't get too intense and ruin the sport for these kids. It was Spence and me and the grandkids, aged 5 and 3. Dad and Grandma were on hand for the grunt work in what would be a glittering team effort.

"Isn't this sort of like asking Jack Nicklaus to teach your kids how to hit a golf ball?" noted the bemused dad, Kevin Coyle. "It's sort of overkill, isn't it?"

Well, maybe. But if you want things done really right. . .

Spence rigged the kids himself like an overindulgent uncle, drawing forth his finest $70 Shimano ultralight rods and matched spinning reels with superfine 2-pound test line. If they were going to learn to fish the right way, he growled, they might as well start with decent gear.

He had leeches for bluegills and medium fathead minnows for any crappie in the area. Spence was being selective. He knew that small to medium bluegills usually reject leeches, but the bigger fish find them irresistible. He wanted big ones, like the 70 huge 'gills his party caught in three hours two days earlier, up to 10½ inches long.

Spence also noticed something nifty at the time, when four large crappie also gulped the leeches. It made him want to see what they also would do with minnows.

On the day before we joined him, he found out. Spence said he had been up all night pacing.

"It was a rare instance in this lake when normally scattered crappie were staging before the spawn," he said. "I hooked one minnow through the lips, and it swam around until a crappie hit it, which meant I located them. I then hooked the other minnows through the back, and since they swim with greater distress, they were quickly taken by crappies."

In 45 minutes, he had 30 big crappie and six huge bluegills on minnows. And these were not ordinary crappie, but trophies of 12 to 13½ inches, fish that stretched from the tip of a finger to midway down the forearm. That evening Spence did it again, catching 10 more huge crappie and five 'gills on minnows.

"It was the best day I've ever had on big crappies in my life," he said.

Spence had noticed some roiling shoreline water where bluegills were building nests. By the time we got there last Sunday, the water had cleared and we could see hundreds of Swiss-cheeselike holes in the mud, many guarded by finning 'gills.

Spence clamped a tiny split shot on the line, hooked a leech onto a small hook and flipped the rig 15 feet.

"Here," he said, handing the elder kid the rod.

It was as easy as that.

They took turns for a while, Jon, 5, and Mike, 3, each feeling the fish pull, learning when to let them run, learning to swing fish ashore with the right length of line.

After a while, the 5-year-old wanted to cast his own bait, so I showed him how to pin the line against the reel base with his index finger, open the bale, gently bring the rod back and let the line go with a little whip. He promptly plopped the bait out there 20 feet with a nice arc, and Spence shrugged: "Pretty soon he'll be doing it on his own."

Just then the kid yelped, "I got one!" And that was it.

After four in a row by himself, all we had to do was extricate the fish, hook whichever leech the kid picked up himself, untangle the line now and then, and leave him alone. Soon he insisted on using "widows," having a little trouble with the word "minnows." By the time he got that corrected to "middows," he was catching bluegills and crappie wherever he cast.

Meanwhile, the 3-year-old was happily casting practice plugs with a tiny spincast reel, and he had begun to flip them well enough that I wondered what he would do with a real hook. So I tied on a Beetle Spin, but that didn't work. He wanted to let the spinner lay in the mud like a leech. I showed him how a retrieve should work, caught a crappie, and the older kid wanted to do that, too. So he began ripping minnows through the water as if they were spinner bait, and it's a good thing he didn't catch any fish that way or my credibility would have sunk.

When young Jon snagged a second tree across the way, Spence beamed, knowing what the kid will endure in years ahead.

"He's becoming a fisherman," he said.

Later came the sweetest words I heard all day: "Grandpa, I got tangled again . . . but I can undo it."

In the end we had 40 huge 'gills of 8½ to 9 inches in the cooler along with a dozen or so crappie up to 13½.

"You sure you've never done this before?" Spence teased the 5-year-old. "Well, you're pretty good. It's not easy to cast a leech and split shot on 2-pound line. I've had more problems with your Grandpa."

So the scenario is complete at last and the kids are spoiled forever. They think this is how fishing always is.

Later, while casting practice plugs off the deck while waiting for the fish to fry, young Jon was asked who did the best.

"I did," he yelped, "because I caught most of the fish."

He was surprised when I shook my head no.

"You were the best?" No again. "Daddy?" Another no.

A grin spread across his face: "I know. Spence was the best because he helped everyone catch the fish."

Pretty smart for a 5-year-old. I think we'll get along.

JOHN HUSAR

April 20, 1994

Turkey hunt wet, cold heaven

Now, I'll admit it. I'll sit right here and wring my socks and grimace if you try to say this turkey business is normal behavior.

Regular folks just don't crawl out of bed at 3 a.m., swallow gobs of fat-boiled food, then slither up muddy farm roads before first light in the midst of a downpour.

I'll admit that. And I won't even contest the apparent nonsense of sliding around a cornfield to make noises that sound more or less like a confused owl. So maybe you'll jar awake a turkey that's still asleep on the branch of an oak tree. So the turkey's not going to come down where you want him, anyway. Or at least, that has been my experience the last couple of years.

I'll never forget last year's hunt near the strip mines of eastern Brown County. For days and days, it poured. This was the beginning of all those floods, remember? I'd been assigned the southern side of a mine road so slick with yellow mud you didn't dare drive it. The only convenient way to my spot seemed to be along a creek that crossed the road through a culvert.

I thought I'd ease down the embankment, make my way to the creek, then walk the bank far enough into the woods to be in turkey country.

In the dimmest predawn light, I saw the winding creek, and I saw the bank-or at least what I thought was bank. In two steps, I was thigh-deep in clay mud. It took all my strength to turn around and "pole" my way free with the butt of my shotgun.

Then came the ugly sucking sensation of my rubber boots coming off. I morosely wheeled around, flopped forward and scoured the mud to find my boots. I pulled them out one by one, slithered back to firm ground, found a rock, sat down and nearly screamed in rage.

Then I did what any turkey hunter would consider perfectly rational. I discarded my socks, cleaned out my boots, cleared my shotgun and squished up the hollow in full daylight, hoping to hear a turkey before it saw me. For four hours in the rain, I futilely tried to make a gobbler-any gobbler-answer my feeble call. And I was happy.

That's the insanity of it all. Turkey hunters enjoy any kind of misery as long as there's half a chance to contact a willing bird. You don't even have to shoot it. Just hearing it answer is enough. I tell folks it's part of being at one with nature, but I really suppose it's some sort of brain disease.

And so it was again last week when Mike Di Rienzo and I hied off to Jo Daviess County for the first of four Illinois spring turkey seasons. We stole through crunchy leaves the first day, hearing hens all around but darned few gobblers. That's the gamble hunters take in early seasons. Although you may be first to reach the birds, they may be too busy to come to your beck and call.

Those early gobblers are captivated by the charms of too many willing hens. They don't even look up when they hear a hunter's sauciest plea.

Unless you are lucky enough to hunker right in the path of a migrating super tom, your best chances are with inexperienced year-old jakes, who either have been chased away by stronger toms or are too stupid to recognize a grungy hunter's sexy bird remarks.

That's what Mike and I encountered the first day—three jakes skirting the edge of our cornfield. They clearly wondered about that racket we were causing in the thicket below. Unfortunately, they weren't gullible enough. While Mike and I crawled forth like Viet Cong guerrillas, the turkeys stayed just out of range.

That's when Mike tried to play his ace. He reached into his game pouch and hauled out a hen decoy he'd been carting around. He flicked the hen here and there, while scratching the ground with his other hand.

The jakes watched incredulously. They must have thought this was the busiest, hungriest, goofiest hen they'd ever seen.

After the jakes had walked away, shaking their heads, Mike turned to me with a scowl on his face.

"Don't you ever mention this to anyone while I'm alive," he hissed. "I couldn't stand my friends smirking at the image of me scratching a decoy after acorns." I solemnly promised to keep his secret—for at least a day.

But at least he tried something, which was better than some of the poor mopes in our group who were confined to blinds by an outfitter whose idea of turkey hunting is to plop as many hunters as possible in likely, confined spots and hope the surrounded birds will run into some of them. That may be fine for absolute neophytes who can't call or if one's legs don't work. But most turkey hunters have this compulsion to sneak after working birds through open woods. That's why it's a sport and not a shoot.

And that's what we were trying to do the next day when a deluge shut down the birds and there was nothing to do but pick a likely spot and sit down and wait like mopes.

Bundled in rain gear, Mike and I lay on the gentle slope of a wooded hillside and watched thick, gray sheets of moisture shield the bottom and shroud the opposite hillside. There was no sound but the drumming rain. We sat in the downpour for an hour and heard nothing else. And we were happy.

July 30, 1986

Shallow thinking brings out the best kings

When Henry Tews finally downed his tea at 7:15 a.m., it tasted mighty sweet.

The tea bag had been lolling in his plastic cup since we'd chugged out of Winthrop Harbor shortly after 6 a.m.

"I have a tradition," Henry had warned before the young chinook came aboard. "I always have a fish in the boat before I finish my first cup of tea."

He cackled contentedly, as befits a man who has stumbled onto a king salmon "honey hole" in Lake Michigan, with salmon abounding in the neighborhood of 15 to 21 pounds.

"I can't believe it," Tews chortled. "Every time I've gone out for two weeks now, they've been right here."

In all that time, Henry has not trolled farther than 500 yards off shore, and he has been virtually alone. The charter captains and other serious fishermen uniformly patrol deeper waters now, often settling for lake trout.Tews has been absolutely unnoticed, hauling 20-pounders into his 22-foot Sea Ray, "Father's Affair."

Henry swigged his tea and gloated, his trim, athletic physique belying a bypass surgery. "There must have been 300 boats out the other day," he said. "Not one was closer to me than three miles."

Tews admits to having no idea why the fish were there, which possibly was why he dragged me along. He figured we'd find out. But first we had to catch more than just one.

Time passed as Henry counseled patience. "We probably came out too early," said the Wheaton print shop owner. "I've been catching almost everything around noon, certainly between 9 a.m. and 2 p.m."

So we bobbed around and waited, checking lines and switching lures until another downrigger popped at last around 9:30 a.m.

This one was mine, and it was a good fish. For a second I'd thought we'd snagged a log or a commercial net. But the fish kept pulling and the line screamed as I eased the drag.

Henry killed the engine, pulled in the other lines and took down the antenna. That was a good thing because the fish hauled me twice around the boat.

We struggled for 25 minutes through a dozen runs, the fish sounding whenever it glimpsed the boat.

I worked the king slowly, gently, enough to feel constant resistance. I'd gain some feet with the reel but quickly lose them, often with interest. The 19-pounder fought until it was totally spent. It finally lay in my cradled arms, lightly hooked in the lip, without the strength to flick a fin. Now, I thought, this is fishing.

We checked our depths, and Henry's steel-blue eyes glimmered with triumph.

"Exactly 32 feet of water," he thundered. "And 24 feet down."

Those, indeed, had been intended to be the magic numbers. For two weeks they had been a closely guarded gift to Henry, and now he was ready to share. "I was at the dock when a guy came in with a load of chinooks," Henry explained. "I asked him where, and he said 34 feet out and 22 feet down, and that was all I needed to know."

Henry never did do much at 34 feet because his rigs began to pop at 32, and that is where he stayed.

He has been trolling a four-mile stretch between Winthrop Harbor and Zion, paying special attention to an electronic booster tower just north ofKellogg Creek. That's where we found our big king and, in fact, most of the fish we took last weekend.

There also was a 15-pound king and a 10-pound wandering laker, plus a number of clean, young 2- and 3-pound salmon—perfect fryers in butter with a touch of onion, garlic and parsley. We boated 10 of 11 fish, losing only one, and most came, as predicted, right around noon.

"I think we made a mistake going out so early," Henry said. "In fact, most guys may be going too deep and too early. By the time they come back from deep water, they're tired and don't think of working the shallows. And the guys who start later miss the best period because they're just starting out and they haven't found the fish."

As to why those fish were there, we can credit the miracle of electronic graphing. We found hordes of fish in water between 32 and 34 feet deep, hovering 22 to 27 feet down. A storm the night before had pushed many more onto the bottom, but they were not striking.

The graph also found a hump off that radio tower dissolving into a 32-foot trench. A narrow, rugged reef then maintains that depth for several hundred feet toward shore. The bottom seems covered with weeds that hold baitfish.

While a couple of other 32-foot trenches radiate through the area, some had fish and others did not. A closer look at the bottom there is in order.

"I'm just guessing, of course, but I don't expect these fish to stay here forever," Henry said. "The winds, the temperature, the weather, all might force a change. But who knows when? They've been here for two weeks despite some lively storms, so I'll just keep fishing them until they move on."

Henry understood that he'd have but a few more days of solitude. By today, of course, he'll hardly be alone.

April 20,1994

Mountain of a man, dad was the model of my sporting life

My father took me fishing just once. I was 4 or 5 when we went in a rowboat on Powers Lake. Dad was gentle when his brave son refused to hook the worm.

He flung this big bobber over what I now figure was a decent weedbed and, after a while, the bobber moved. Dad made me jerk the rod and, lo, I reeled in my first fish.

The bluegill was tiny, and very angry. Dad tried to show me how to hold the fish, but I wouldn't touch it. He cast again, but the bluegills weren't interested. After what seemed like endless hours in the blazing sun, but probably was no more than half an hour, Mom indicated it was time to go. One fish, that was it.

I think Dad was glad I wasn't going to be an avid fishing companion. He needed time to be by himself. I remember him slipping away in the evenings, unchaining the wooden boat, rowing by himself to the weedbed. He'd stay out there for hours, his cigarette glowing on the water, sometimes long after my cousin Tom and I had gone to bed.

He must have done all right. We soon had a fish fry, an immense platter of sweet, crispy fillets. I'd never tasted anything so good, and Dad was proud.

One night Dad heroically removed a black snake from the bed my cousin and I shared. Then Dad and Uncle Lou made us kids crawl back in. I think they promised to stand guard through the night. We fell asleep as sounds of pinochle drifted up the stairs.

And that was it for Dad and me in the outdoors. You could have blown him over with a feather the day I got this outdoor writing job. "Tell me, just what do you know about this stuff?" he demanded.

"About as much as I had to know to cover football and golf," I replied.

That was another joke to him, for it was Dad who should have been the sportswriter. In 29 years at this paper, I've never met a person who knew more than him about the history and soul of sports.

He was a great amateur player in his day, a seven-letterman in three sports at Purdue, a starting center on the Boilermakers' 1932 national basketball championship team with Johnny Wooden. He was a tough, mean player nicknamed "Firpo" after the boxer. When I ran into Wooden for a story I was doing on the West Coast, all he wanted to talk about was how tough was my dad.

I'll tell you how tough he could be with me. The day before I left for college on a football scholarship, Dad took me out in back, got into a defensive crouch and growled: "Block me."

Block my dad? This old guy who worked in a factory after my summer of lifting weights? "Aw, c'mon, Dad," I begged, but he insisted.

So I blocked him, or maybe it was the side of the house the way my head was reeling. I was nose-down in the grass, while Dad still hovered there in his crouch.

"Now block me again," he barked.

Eleven times I tried, and 11 times my bones were trashed to powder. I knew I'd never get to school, never get out of that yard, until I just once blocked Dad.

So I threw a dirty block. A crackback, a clip. And he took it and nodded, and let me go back in the house. He figured I'd survive.

Years later, when arthritis had confined him to a walker, I often wondered if that dirty knee block had played a role. Dad said it hadn't. He'd played on broken bones in the era of soft leather helmets. That's how I nailed him in later life. Whenever he'd be irascibly hard-headed about something, I'd sorrowfully nod to my brothers about how sad it was that Dad had to suffer from playing with a helmet he could fold up and carry in his pocket.

Dad stayed in sports by umpiring ballgames around the city, and in the fall he'd make big bucks, like $10, refereeing sandlot football. He'd be the only ref on the field, calling offsides, illegal motion, holding and roughness while somehow following the play and keeping time. I'd tag along as a little kid and marvel at all the things he could see. He taught me the keys of watching football.

I loved to go with him to softball games, to carry the equipment bag of a man in blue. City bus drivers, who know something of the hassle umpires face, treated him respectfully.

Dad brought along his own foul line flags and a little hammer to stake them down. He carried spiked shoes, a whisk broom, a face mask and an inflatable chest protector for baseball. As the umpire's kid, I got to sit on the team benches, although Dad made me switch sides at midpoint and told me never to cheer one team only. My biggest thrills occurred during the arguments, with Dad towering over the furious players, and I exulted when he'd toss 'em out. My dad always won.

After the games, I got to star in another ritual. When Dad called the final out, I'd spring down the nearest foul line, snatch his flag, then race across the outfield to the other flag. If I didn't, someone would steal them, for sure.

These were just some of the memories that flooded back when we went through Dad's things after the funeral. We all pocketed sweet mementoes. Mine included the remnants of an old sleeve of rusty snelled hooks, No. 6s, perfect for bluegills. They had to be 50 years old.

And I snagged an old, creased umpire's shirt patch with four over-sized safety pins. Dad owned only one patch, so he'd pin it each time onto a clean blue shirt.

CHAPTER TWO
MORNING SUN

*Before John Husar arrived on the scene, newspaper out-
door columns for the most part were about hooks and bullets,
focusing on where to catch the biggest fish, find the most
pheasants and how to track and kill a trophy deer.*

*John liked catching big fish as much as anyone else, but he
understood that there were thousands of people among his
readers who didn't care to bait a hook or squeeze a trigger.
So he wrote for them, too.*

*He took them snowmobiling in the Arctic, sailboarding in
Oregon. A hike into the Grand Canyon, a horseback ride
with a governor or a wading trip down a local river was just
as grand an adventure to John as an international safari—
maybe even more so. He embraced newfangled participatory
sports like mountain biking as eagerly as he cast lures to
hungry walleye.*

*Sometimes longtime hunters and anglers complained that
John spent too much time on these other sports. John gave
them short shrift. He knew there was room for everyone in
the great outdoors.*

August 4, 1993

Well worth the walk

GRAND CANYON VILLAGE, Ariz.—Fifteen-hundred feet below the South Rim, you are far enough into the Grand Canyon.

You've lurched and skidded maybe a mile and a half. The flat rim towers above, and you've trekked beside the rare stand of Douglas fir that hugs the coolest and shadiest side of the gorge.

At the announced rate of 20,000 years for each step in a place that exposes 2 billion years of time, you've probably traversed 600,000 years. Not bad for a leisurely hour's work.

You've passed through the limestone and sandstone layers, and now you're sitting on a flat stem of russet shale, feet dangling into nowhere, the canyon thrusting its rocky images and palette of colors straight into your face.

That's as far as you need to go. Sure, you can hike farther. You can continue a few more miles and another thousand or so feet downward and walk across the smooth, sculpted desert of the lower Tonto Plateau until you peer directly into the steep black inner gorge that shields the Colorado River from most eyes searching from the rim.

You can go the full 8 miles if you wish, if you are carrying enough water, all the way to the bunkhouses of Phantom Ranch at the bottom, a mile below the rim. There you can stay with the mules and handful of other overnight tourists who are of sound enough body and spirit to test themselves on these wondrous trails.

Or you can sit right here until sunset, just one-third of the way down—hovering in space, it seems, on a shelf beside the South Kaibab Trail.

This is the trail of choice for Grand Canyon National Park staffers. Most of the 5 million annual visitors cluster around the mouth of Bright Angel Trail nearest the lodges, and some even saunter a mile or three to maintained water stations. Those who pride their rugged-ness go farther west to Hermit's Rest to hike a much tougher route with no watering spots. But insiders head east toward Yaki Point, where the South Kaibab quickly turns a spectacular series of zigzag switchbacks into the most revealing sight that most Canyon visitors ever will see.

Jim Tuck, the park's assistant superintendent, says the other trails are confined too long in deep bays, the view sheltered by narrow points. You must hike a long way to be surrounded by open beauty. "But the South Kaibab opens up quickly and you are right in the middle of things," Tuck said. "That's where most of us take a walk after work. Besides, there's maybe one-third the people there."

Sadly, most of the 5 million visitors never experience the full impact of the world's most revered canyon. Only a tiny fraction penetrate the immensely rugged, arid and dangerous back country beyond the maintained trails. "Most people don't venture there. Most people shouldn't venture there," said Ranger Kathy Dascoll, a native of Chicago's Hyde Park community.

But unless a person is hopelessly out of shape, he or she should try to get somewhat into the canyon, she said. Only then can one begin to understand its profound historic and geologic implications, the immensity of its nature, and to float in the womb of its ageless grandeur.

"People think they experience the canyon when they come and look for a few minutes," Dascoll said. "It's like the movie *National Lampoon's Vacation*. Chevy Chase brings his family to the canyon. 'Well, gang, here it is. Let's go,' he says. That's the perfect parody."

Most stays here are woefully short, four or five hours. Only one of 10 visitors enjoys a short hike, usually on a nature trail. Less than 1 percent of those go farther.

Most are daunted by the lack of water. "It's the most critical thing you can bring along," Dascoll said. "Hikers lose a quart of water each hour. In this dryness, people don't realize they're sweating that much, and if they don't replenish that water they can get into trouble. We average one death a year from heatstroke, plus several hundred cases of heat exhaustion."

Rangers recommend three quarts on a downhill trip and at least a gallon on the hike back up. Most hikes average four to five hours down and eight to 10 hours out. For prolonged backpacking, for which a permit is required, Dascoll urges hikers to think ultralight.

"Most people bring far too much gear," she said. "You generally don't need a tent.

"You don't need a stove and pots and pans. You don't really need a hot meal every day. I precook a meal of onions, green chili, beans and salsa and freeze it in a plastic container. It's thawed by the time I'm hungry. You can bring peanut butter and jelly, high-energy gorp or survive for a few days on dried milk and cereal."

Other "don'ts" are excessive clothes—the same grungy T-shirt is fine for four days; no one cares—heavy fresh fruits, extra books or field guides, heavy leather hiking boots, superfluous makeup, even deodorant.

"Everything you pack in, you pack out," Dascoll warned. "The things people leave behind at Phantom Ranch are hilarious. Brand-new boots that gave them blisters, hair curlers, blow dryers, rain gear. I saw one fellow go down with a lawn chair strapped to his pack."

Of course, little but water is needed for short sojourns like mine, only a third of the way down. A few dozen others also had made the trip, most heading straight back up. I stayed as long as the light held, outwaiting even a ranger, wanting to be last one out.

The hike up was stunning. At each turn, the changing light painted the sheer walls in new shades from amber to ochre until night finally enveloped the canyon, a silver half-moon and cobalt sky illuminating my trail.

Of 5 million Grand Canyon visitors, I had become statistically one of 50,000. And now I was the only one left on the trail.

September 25, 1997

Columbia Gorge flips over sailboards

HOOD RIVER, Ore.—Wiry, charismatic Doug Campbell had just moved to Portland to practice medicine in 1980 when someone talked him into trying a new demo sailboard.

"I had never seen one before," he recalled the other day. "I immediately bought two."

He became the pioneer who changed the face of this old orchard and logging community beside the vast Columbia River. Campbell's inadvertent revolution turned sleepy old Hood River into the continental Mecca for sailboarding—just as Albuquerque is for ballooning, Eugene, Ore., for running and Oshkosh, Wis., for antique airplanes. While Maui in the Pacific Ocean may have more glamour and bigger waves, Hood River rules the Lower 48.

Campbell discovered unique sailing conditions in the peculiar winds and currents of the scenic Columbia Gorge—a massive wind tunnel carved by erosion through the Cascade Mountains. When the Columbia's strong, steady, sea-bound current collides with stiff winds from the ocean, huge swells arise in a 100-mile reach—and especially around Hood River.

These 5- and 6-foot swells lift boardsailers into quartering winds that permit spectacular turns, jumps and flips. Then these wondrously accommodating winds triangulate them back to where they started to catch another swell and do it all over again, day in and day out, from April through September.

When Campbell first rode the Columbia's magnificent swells, there

21

wasn't a single stoplight in Hood River. Nowadays, thousands of so-called "boardheads" clog the town, spawning Aspen-like boutiques and jacking up property values to the point of displacing many disgruntled locals. Virtually half the stores in the old downtown beside the river are owned by boardheads or those catering to them. The phone book lists 47 sail and equipment shops in the Columbia Gorge, with 26 in Hood River itself. Most offer rentals and lessons.

"We've become like a ski town," said Peter Lake, one of a dozen or more Chicagoans who have migrated here. "Except the season's reversed."

Hood River's boardsailing industry has capitalized upon a mass of maturing aficionados who come from everywhere with pockets stuffed with money. Older boardheads boast how they enjoy more of the quiet joys of windsurfing than the hair-raising thrills that once turned them on. This metamorphosis has broadened windsurfing well beyond the realm of "extreme" sports that gave it birth—and draws big money into the business.

Hood River also has the unique advantage of being prime country for many other "edgy" outdoor recreation sports that have been driven by the fitness and adventure booms in America. Windsurfing now shares local billing with mountain bikes, kayaks, sailboats, paragliders, various types of skiers, not to mention the climbers and hikers who scurry up and down nearby Mt. Hood.

Snowboards ply the mountain's corn snow through September. Hikers circulate amid 150 waterfalls in nearby state and national forests. The 2-year-old Timberland Gorge Games now is a week full of cutting-edge events each July—complete with top pros—in windsurfing, mountain biking, 49er-class sailing, snowboarding, kayaking, outrigger canoeing, paragliding, kiteskiing as well as the inevitable running and climbing.

"So you can see the choices that people have around here," said Pete Fotheringham, publisher of the Columbia Gorge Visitor and Recreation Guide. "If the wind doesn't blow, you always can go mountain biking or skiing. Some people around here believe a good day in Hood River is a three-sport day—skiing in the morning, biking in the afternoon and boardsailing in the evening."

When Campbell—who gave up his medical practice to open a board shop and dabble in other enterprises—began having small slaloms and minor competitive events for friends and newcomers to the sport in 1982, boardsailing focused on zany acts of daring. Magazines carried nothing but photos of jumpers and loopers. Videos extolled extreme techniques. Hood River became the scene for longhaired, raggedy, youthful surf bums who slept in vans, parks and beneath bridges, carting their boards atop their vehicles.

But times changed as boardsailing grew up. The prime market now concerns $3,000 startup rigs for aging yuppies with bulging salaries who think nothing of owning three or four boards of different lengths and six or seven specialized sails for varying wind conditions. Wet suits sell for hundreds of dollars, specialized gloves for $30, snazzy caps for $15.

Hood River landlords found gold mines in seasonal condominium rentals, coffee bars and cafes with $7 omelets. Three years ago, the mayor, city manager and five council members were boardheads—clear acceptance of the sport's annual $20 million-plus economic infusion.

Money was poured into launch sites to the point where Hood River and a matching stretch along the Columbia's Washington shoreline boasts 24 sailboard launch sites, including historic "Doug's Beach," where Campbell started this whole thing. One spectator-friendly spot near the business center simply is called The Event Site, complete with sloping grassy shoreline and grandstands.

"What happened was the industry discovered it had made a mistake in focusing upon the 18-year-old kid in Maui who can fly off a wave," said 60-ish David Hmiel, who ended 10 years of four-hour commutes from Seattle when he and his wife moved to Hood River after retirement.

"It found that's not where the money is. The money is you and me— and our children. Go down to the shoreline and you'll see a lot of gray hair around. I'll bet no more than 2 percent of the boardheads today actually do any loops."

Instead, the industry found a huge market in people who just love to ride the wind, and who are willing to sacrifice to be as close as possible to prime sailing conditions.

"Basically, we don't go windsurfing because we want to," Hmiel said. "We go because we have to."

Naturally, such rapid reversal of community patterns has driven a social wedge through Hood River. The estimated 85 percent of natives who never have windsurfed justifiably resent the housing and restaurant price jumps that have pushed most of them toward a grittier second downtown a couple of miles beyond the rim of the town's scenic bluffs. Locals working for standard wages just cannot afford bluffside views.

"Overall, the economy has changed," confirmed Carol York, the only county commissioner who is involved in the boardsailing business. "But you can't say it has been bad for this area. A lot of things are happening here. For many people, this has become the choice place to live."

She gave a small sigh.

"Fifteen years ago, you couldn't go out to eat on Sunday or Monday except to one 24-hour diner."

JOHN HUSAR

November 30, 1997

Room with a view, comforts of home

Poor Louise. She seems to think one of her wifely obligations is to hunt deer.

Ever since the first time she gamely raised a shotgun at a button buck and actually killed the animal, she felt locked into this annual ritual. Sitting in predawn darkness beneath some soggy tree seemed to her a sort of punishment for being an outdoor writer's wife.

"Just don't you ever write about me again," she hissed.

I lamely smiled. You see, this kid makes such good copy. . . .

* * *

Four of us were having lunch at Turkey Trot Rod & Gun Club when Louise clomped into the clubhouse on the second day of deer season, looking for her chickens.

Americo, who raises everything from peacocks, geese and turkeys to guinea hens, muscovies and pigeons in the pheasant pens behind the barn—everything but pheasant—was going to give her enough birds to start a flock at our little cabin a few miles away.

Louise poured some coffee and absorbed our tales of woe. So far, five of us had bagged just one deer. Our spirits were flagging.

I had begun to kick myself for letting go the biggest buck I ever had seen at Turkey Trot just because the darned thing showed up in dim light before legal shooting hours and I didn't have a certain, killing shot. But, of course, you don't risk wounding a buck like that. So I let it go—and, although I had seen 13 other deer, that one never came back.

Louise tried to make us feel a little better.

"Well, I'm going to have to turn in my wedding ring," she kidded.

Then she spilled her own deer-hunting misfortunes.

It seems that while we were sitting in cold, damp dawnlight, mistaking sounds of squirrels for deer, Louise was in comfy pajamas, having a second cup of coffee at the cabin. She had decided not to expose her cough to the dampness—a nice, civilized excuse to stay inside.

"There I was, sitting back in the recliner, reading yesterday's papers, the radio playing classical music," she said. "All that coffee made me have to go to the bathroom. When I got there, I looked out the window and saw these two deer standing halfway down the hill, just behind the deck."

Louise ran toward the front door for her shotgun, clicked in a couple of slugs, then happened to glance outside and see three more deer standing in the side yard beside the hammock.

Intending to be as legal as possible, she clamped an orange cap on her head, opened the door, took one step out and fired at the biggest deer.

"And I missed," she sighed. "All three just kept standing there. They were looking around to see what was going on."

Now she was in a panic. She raced back to the bathroom only to see the first two deer still in the same spot.

She slid open the picture window—the same window from which our son-in-law had killed a deer last year while answering a call of nature. Louise sat on a tall chair and waited for the deer to move. When the big doe eventually stepped from the shelter of the deck, Louise drew a bead and fired.

"And I missed!" she bleated.

She watched the deer turn and slowly walk away.

Meanwhile, the dog bolted through the half-opened front door and ran downhill to retrieve whatever there might be to retrieve. When Louise went to call her, those three front-yard deer still looked her over from the hammock.

So, she shot again. And missed again. The deer finally jumped over the fence.

"You should have seen me." Louise said. "I was running around the cabin like Elmer Fudd with the '1812 Overture' playing on the radio."

Now she just wanted to collect her promised chickens. Like any kindly men, we gave her copious advice on how to practice her shooting.

We all assured her she had done an admirable job.

"At least you took some shots," said Robbie Brown, who had let a few deer pass because he wanted a big one with his muzzle-loader.

"We haven't done all that well around here," I conceded.

Louise wrinkled her nose.

"Well, you always could come home and sit in the bathroom for a while," she muttered.

I went with her to the cabin to spread some hay and put the chickens into a mesh silo she had prepared. By the time the work was done, it was too late to drive back to the club to hunt that afternoon, so I went down the hill to a tall, hollow half-stump near the creek, where deer often pass near the cabin.

Three came by, but none was within range. One seemed to be limping, hanging back, and I wondered if it had been wounded.

On my way up the hill at sunset, I kept looking in the direction those deer had gone, hoping to see one bedding where I could find it in the morning.

Then I saw this patch of brown and white in a hollow beside the pond road. It was a big doe, body stiff, cool to the touch, dead for several hours. A blood trail led uphill toward our cabin's deck.

Inside the cabin, Louise was curled up in a chair.

"You aren't as bad a shot as you think," I informed her, telling what I had found.

"No way," she declared. "If I had hit that deer, it would have to be on the left side."

When she brought the four-wheeler down the hill and leaned across the doe, the slug hole clearly was on the left side. This deer had bled to death in minutes.

"Didn't you watch it walk away?" I testily demanded. "Didn't you wait to see where it went?"

She miserably shook her head.

"I just didn't think I hit it," she said.

I spent the next morning checking our property as well as the neighbor's for signs of a second doe, but Louise was off the hook. The dog only found some long-dead coyote-riddled bones that none of us had known about.

When I got back to the cabin, the tall chair—now draped in camouflage—had been dragged back to the bathroom window. An orange hat waited nearby.

This was the ultimate courtesy among deer hunters. Louise was offering me her blind.

February 19, 1989

A snowmobiling trip to a land of wonder

FAIRPLAY, COLO.—You'd understand why I've been having trouble keeping my eyes on business.

For the map room of the beautifully restored 11-room Hand Hotel overlooks the jagged peaks of the gold-rich Mosquito Range.

I am scrunched in the snugness of a plush sofa, tracing with a finger the mountain Jeep and mining trails on Colorado topo maps, all the while feasting an eye upon the very mountains embraced by those trails.

Through the window and across a snowy sundeck, a white mountain meadow sweeps broadly beyond the trout-rich middle fork of the South Platte River, here a tiny stream encased in ice.

One lone elk track crosses the stream to range within 30 yards of our back door. It backs up and winds through some thin scrub toward the green fringe of spruce that circles the snowy domes of these mountains like the cropped rim of a bald man's head.

From this old, springy sofa, I've been dreaming of planting a foot upon each of the handful of 14,000-footers within view. From this window at 10,000 feet, they seem close, accessible. And the maps with the trails are right here in the antique bookcase, the coffee is hot, the beer is cold . . . ah, well.

It still is winter, and at this level of Colorado they have eight or nine months of it. Only loony flatlanders such as myself let their imaginations brave the snowswept alpine tundra above the treeline for very long at this time of year.

Of course, if you could get your hands on some snowmobiles . . .

Downstairs, addled by the crackling logs in the fireplace, Sage Greising lets a merry sparkle flash through his brown eyes. The transplanted Chicagoan, now mayor of this near ghost town of 530 at the top of the world, announces that a good snowmobiler can scale a certain three nearby 14,000-foot peaks in a single day "if, of course, you know the way."

And Griesing does—or claims to—but it is much too late in this particular day for him to settle that magnificent boast.

"But I can still show you something wonderful," he says, and is off to gas his machines.

Soon we are unloading three snowmobiles at the Beaver Creek access area to Pike National Forest, three miles out of town, where one other car sits in the frozen lot. And then we are zooming through huge fields of deep powder, nearly bogging in the unexpected lightness-skidding, sliding, almost flying.

We cross a snow-buried campground and rise through the forest along a narrow creek bank, emerging through snow-sealed grassy mountain meadows. Elk and bighorn sheep tracks are everywhere.

Sage stops his machine and walks back for a word.

"Keep a little left," he instructs. My wife, Louise, has never been on a snowmobile before, but I think he means me. "Lean, if you have to. You don't want to slide into the creek."

A few miles later, just below the treeline around 12,000 feet, he comes back again.

"Now we go almost straight up the hill," he says. "You'll have to accelerate much faster than we've been going. Just don't get the sled turned sideways on the hill."

We had no trouble imagining a sled-sized snowball tumbling down the mountain.

But we easily vroomed uphill until Sage turned and stopped on the edge of a snowy flat and beckoned us off the machines. Just a few feet higher rose the bald crest of a gravelly, rocky hill called Beaver Ridge. The snowpack stopped here, blown away by fierce winds.

"Just keep watching ahead of you as you walk up," Sage said. We caught the excitement rising in his voice. "Don't look anywhere else.

Just watch the country reveal itself."

Panting from the high elevation, we eased up the powdery brown gravel and exposed broken rock. As we topped the rise, the land before us fell away for a hundred miles.

"My God," was about all that we could say.

Straight ahead, the vast South Park basin opened as far south as we could see. Our little town of Fairplay was snuggled far below. On one side, the huge Mosquito Range tumbled into the Buffalo Range and then off to become the Sangre de Cristos and run into New Mexico. On our left rose the Tarryalls, blocking the Front Range and Pike's Peak miles away.

We walked around with arms out, embracing the splendor. "I want to sing something from *The Sound of Music*," Louise said.

We noticed the green and orange tundra mosses thinly clinging to the rocks, just as in the Arctic. Behind rose the white peaks of Silverheels and Bross mountains. Between them, hundreds of feet below us, tiny cars chugged through what once had seemed a formidable Hoosier Pass.

"I come up here maybe once a week, sometimes for the sunrise," Sage said with a deep, fulfilled breath. He drew us to the sand-smoothed trunk of a scarred and deformed bristlecone pine tree that leaned, like all the others, sharply from the wind. He slipped off a glove and fondled the living wood.

"Touch it, see how the grains of sand have smoothed it," Sage said, and the moss-colored tree bark felt as though it had been planed.

A former biologist, Sage explained that these wind-deformed bristlecones are the oldest known living creatures. Somehow, they are the only trees of substance that can exist in the grassless alpine tundra above the treeline, and only in very special places.

Across the valley on a wind-swept bald knob alongside Mt. Bross, lies the federal Bristlecone Pine Scenic Area with dwarfed trees as old as 1,800 years, although one in California reportedly is 4,500 years old. Here, though, the trees are unprotected, and some locals, unbelievably, chop them down for cordwood because they burn so long and well.

"Next to these, sequoias are infants," Sage murmured, slipping his glove back on.

Although Sage said he's never camped here, we could see some likely spots protected from the wind and made a promise to return in fall or summer, when the Jeeps can get through. We'll bring a tent and some food, though we doubt we'll have much trouble finding a trout or two in Beaver Creek.

And now we're back in the map room of the Hand Hotel, marking trails, staring at the mountains, dreaming on. The aroma of fresh coffee drifts upstairs. Those peaks indeed are close . . . so touchable . . . so much more so now.

CHAPTER THREE
CLOUDY WEATHER

Some 15 years ahead of Sept. 11, when America suddenly felt less safe, John wrote a Sunday story about a place "no modern would dream of terrorizing." That would be the Canadian Arctic, where 10 degrees Fahrenheit on the thermometer with a strong wind would be a typical day in May—and pause for unzipping your outer parka a few inches.

One of John's enduring gifts to readers is his honesty in print. He would regale us regularly with his love of the snow—every new accumulation was an excuse to pull out the trusty snowshoes—while many of us adults would mutter under our breath about driving through rush-hour slush-ice-sleet-snow. Of course, every Chicago kid would side with John.

On the other hand, he would mention regularly the image of rain getting into his rubber boots, and with no great fondness for the sensation. He would admit surprise in not anticipating a sudden storm while fishing on a river. He lamented cold temperatures when warmer weather would be better for the hunt, or vice versa.

But "Cloudy Weather" didn't deter John. This chapter is proof.

December 28, 1988

A present that can't be wrapped

My Christmas arrived Monday in the form of 6 inches of snow in my corner of the Cook County woods.

While electronic weatherpersons babbled incoherently about the "frightening" snowstorm, I was in the garage, checking the bindings on my snowshoes. And soon I was alone in the snowy stillness, tracing fresh deer tracks through the thickets.

We rarely get enough snow here for serious mushing, and it rarely lasts very long. I wasn't going to miss this chance.

I'd heard only one weatherperson who had the situation right, a guy on WBBM noting the deep, powdery snow was a special gift for kids who received sleds for Christmas. And, of course, the woods were full of parents and laughing children.

But these forest preserves with their 65,000 acres have many untrammeled places off the horsepaths and far from the gaiety of sledding hills. With snowshoes, you can get away. I often find spots that I've never seen before, since fresh snow highlights the tiniest wildlife trails. And, of course, with snowshoes you have no trouble following those trails.

This time when I left the horsepath, I circled some thick hawthorns that shielded a grand meadow and picked up some fresher tracks. The wind was in my face, and so there was a chance that I could surprise some deer without being scented.

The trail wound through a tunnel of trees and shrubs, and from time to time I'd stop to savor the utter silence. There is no better time to be outdoors and alone. Even in Cook County, just 25 minutes from the Loop, there can be an illusion of northern Wisconsin.

The trail branched several times and the deer tracks moved uphill, so I circled halfway around. On one side, I came upon a broad prairie basin leading toward a pair of lakes. No one else was around.

Step by step, I edged silently uphill and came into an upland meadow that, as usual, I hadn't known was there. I waited and listened and then came the crack of wood as two whitetails leaped from a low copse of trees and cut across my direction.

They ran toward some larger trees and then I looked again, for they had run into an oak savanna that was another surprise.

Savannas are increasingly rare forms of open woodland, of large trees in a meadowlike setting. This one sat upon a hill, guarded from the sightlines of distant horsepaths by the woody edge of tall brush. I'd walked and run those horsepaths for 12 years, but it took a pair of deer to introduce me to this wondrous little savanna just a mile or so from the house. I'll go there many, many times.

I stayed for an hour, trapped by the splendid view, while a fresh cushion of snow floated down. I leaned against a tree and watched the colors change as evening came. Three young deer emerged from a circle of forest into the valley below and played all the way across, snapping at bark, jumping at each other, dashing one way and then the next.

A nearby movement caught my eye, two gray hind legs easing behind a tree. Could it be a buck?

I waited and watched and listened hard but heard nothing. I moved closer to the edge of the trees, and then I heard the snort and the rustle and saw the big horns disappearing through some brush. That buck had been tracking me.

It was nearly night now, and the snow had turned to sleet, then light rain. The woods had been protective and I was warm and slightly sweaty. The snow and the low clouds reflected almost enough light for reading. I'd have no trouble getting out.

I followed some new trails in the general direction of the truck. They turned and twisted and came together but there was always one that headed north. Sometimes I had to duck and once I had to crawl to avoid some thorns, but that happens when you follow deer instead of people.

I was still pushing that buck and another deer that had joined the chase. I followed them across a creek, crunching through a thin crust of ice, then saw where the deer had angled through a thin corridor of trees as straight as an arrow flies. I listened, but the woods were quiet.

In another block, a streetlight rudely glimmered through the empty branches. I slowed to make the walk last longer. The woods were bright with snow and reflected cloudlight. But with the rain making the snow heavier, it was a good time to come out.

The weather had given us a rare taste of old-fashioned winter. It's been three winters since we've had a snow like that–deep and powdery and silent.

Twelve hours was all we had before things melted and crusted up, and then came another rain. Around here, we have to take it when we can.

JOHN HUSAR

April 12, 1989

This lake defies the infamous weather hex

My fishing calendar, otherwise known as the Kiss of Death, is infamous for untimely timing.

Possibly half my trips occur during the worst possible weather. I rarely leave home unless a cold front is occurring or predicted.

The one time I thought I might be exempt was in the stable patterns of the Canadian High Arctic, and then I managed to fall through the ice.

My fishing calendar is responsible for hurricanes and tornadoes. My friends generally note when I am going somewhere and plan their trip for the week before.

On Sunday, some buddies were determined to prove that weather shouldn't matter. They believe that fish must eat, even when I am fishing. They wanted to show that we—okay, I—could catch fish under the worst weather conditions and therefore no longer could blame the weather. They were determined to strip me of my last excuse. They and my schedule conspired for the perfect springtime day.

It snowed as we left Chicago, and the wind picked up nicely on the way. By the time we reached Aldo Marchetti's hideaway in western Illinois, whitecaps were frothing on the surface of the little lake. It was 28 degrees, and that doesn't count the chill. Suffice to say that beads of ice had formed on the windshield of the truck.

"I wasn't prepared for this," grumped Bill Cullerton as he added his third layer of mittens. Black clouds rose in the west as we pushed the little jon boat off the beach.

"Hmm, not bad," Aldo said. "This morning I couldn't even get it to move in the wind." He said he had to jump in and push the boat far enough for the trolling motor to do some good. Then he found a school of fish. And he caught some, just to prove a point.

"That's why I have you guys out here," Aldo bellowed through the wind. "These are the most despicable conditions that I can think of. They're obscene. And now we're going to catch some fish."

The little boat nudged the wind until we were over 40 feet of water, a typical depth for a flooded quarry. We switched on a pair of liquid crystal graphs—one fore, the other aft—to see what these waters were holding.

In 43 and 44 feet, the fish began appearing. Schools were suspended at varying levels. Nothing would appeal to them. Then we saw the black humps on the bottom.

"Those fish on the bottom are hungry," Aldo said. "Let's get 'em."

We rigged small jigging Rapalas with uni-knots to short, tippy crappie rods and small spincast reels. Loops were left in the lines to allow the lures to wobble nicely on the drops. Within 10 minutes, I had a walleye.

"That's because we gave you the best color," Aldo smirked. "Sportswriters always get the best baits."

"As it should be," I concurred, moving to the next grand sportswriter tradition, breaking off the lure on an underwater snag.

Since the three of us had steady hits from walleyes and crappies on eighth-to sixteenth-ounce Raps, I opted for something heavier, to get my lure down straighter and faster. That was a quarter-ounce jigging Rap on a short, stiff Johnson "brush" rod and, bingo, it soon caught two nice crappies, plus another walleye.

"I can't believe you're using anything that heavy," Cullerton said. I told him it was the only way in this wind to feel the bottom.

By now the snow had reached blizzard form, and we were taking crappies from a wall between 28 and 43 feet deep. We let the wind push us toward the bay that held our beach. But before we could haul our icy hands ashore, Aldo had one more point to make.

The graphs varied between 17 and 18 feet, just 10 yards off a point where some insane beavers had girdled trees with two-foot trunks, trying to dam the entire bay.

"There's a weedbed down there," Aldo reported. We scraped it with our jigging Raps and pulled in two perch and a pair of largemouth bass.

As we tied the boat to the beach, Aldo bubbled with pride.

"Remember," he said. "This is the kind of day you don't go out because you can't catch any fish. And we did it without live bait."

In less than two hours, we'd caught 10 good crappies, half a dozen walleyes, three perch and four or five bass.

Of course, we did have some unfair advantages. Aldo had braved the foul morning to make sure he could find fish. I also happened to be sitting beside the designer of one of the first stiff "brush" rods, whose presence was encouragement enough.

"When the government first flooded Toledo Bend and Kentucky Lake some 20-25 years ago, there was still a lot of flooded timber on the bottom," Cullerton explained. "The natives started what they called 'doodle-socking,' which was to 'doodle' a lure through the branches and along the trunk, whereupon they'd 'sock' the bass. When they discovered crappies clustered in those trees and brushpiles, they needed a short rod."

Cullerton said he ordered a manufacturer to begin making solid glass 2-foot rods "and the guy thought I was crazy. I wound up selling 2,000 to 3,000 at a time. It took off from there. Now they're graphite, and they're great for ice fishing, especially lake trout deep, when you have to mount a reel."

We also had some devilishly sharp hooks on those jigging Raps, which enabled us to snag a couple of our fish.

"Hook-making remains one of the secrets of our industry," Cullerton noted. "I've been in factories where the machinery was totally covered. All you see is wire going in one end and a river of hooks pouring out the other.

"Swivels are the same way. The machines are covered, and brass and wire go in one end and swivels pour out the other. Some of these machines have never had patents because no one has ever seen 'em. All of the employees have been there 25–30 years. It's all very secret."

There was no secret, though, to Aldo's smirk.

"In a week or two, when they're on, we'll fill a bucket with crappies off these jigging Raps," he said. "Most people don't know what fantastic lures these are for difficult conditions, and not just for ice fishing."

Cullerton cleared his throat. "Of course, the success of a trip isn't counted by the number of fish in the bucket," he philosophized.

Then he shook his head at Aldo, now feverishly cleaning the crappies as the wind howled and the April snow blew a tantrum. "Except he'd blow his brains out if he ever didn't get any fish."

January 9, 1994

You, too, can canoe
Chicago River in January

Canoeing on New Year's Day. Now, that's a trip to chew on.

Maybe in Georgia or Florida, you say? Where the water at least comes in liquid form?

C'mon, now. We're talking macho. This is about northern Illinois, and specifically the North Branch of the good old Chicago River.

You didn't believe people did this, did you? Well, neither did I until Vic Hurtowy phoned from the Chicagoland Canoe Base to say there would be room on the morning of Jan. 1 in his 18-foot Canadian.

"Vic, you've been drinking, right?" was my first and most plausible reaction.

But, no, it turns out Hurtowy and several disciples of vaunted canoeing fanatic Ralph Frese have done this for nine years—ever since the ongoing river cleanup began showing tangible results.

"You're gonna love it," Hurtowy promised. "Of course, that's if you don't drown or freeze."

So there we were on a crisp and even mildly sunny morning, layered to the gills. Rubber boots and rubber gloves. Meanwhile, people nibbled Christmas cookies from canisters while aligning a string of canoes and kayaks along a forest preserve lane below the dam off Willow Road near Northfield. We would paddle 7 1/2 miles to Linne Woods on Dempster Street.

Because the day was so sweltering—like, maybe 35 degrees—50 people arrived with broad smiles, dragging 30 boats. They ranged in age from 6 to 75, and all seemed fairly competent. At least, no one was trailing straps from any straitjacket, as far as I could tell.

I wondered about the bearded fellow who dressed his canoe in red bows and evergreen bunting and paddled around in circles, but Vic said he was trying to reflect the holiday spirit.

After shuttling cars and vans to our destination, we eased into the stream around 11 a.m.

"This is really terrific weather," Vic gushed. "Last year it was 8 degrees."

The paddling was splendid, despite occasional grinding sandbars. Sometimes you had to search for the narrow channel. A few folks had poled and paddled the route the day before, to make sure it was open. You never can tell about Cook County's streams. Forest preserve efforts to keep streams snag-free and clear of fallen trees are tepid at best. Vic and others spotted several snags officials had reported clear.

Our route traversed long, wooded corridors with gentle bluffs, giant cottonwoods and occasional restored prairie. Twice we spotted deer, and once we were challenged by a stomping buck.

We kept spooking a large flock of mallards that didn't get the hang of what we were doing. They would lunge ahead, out of sight, only to be startled when we would glide around a bend. All they had to do was fly behind us and settle down, but they never figured it out.

A broad vista opened through Chick Evans Golf Course, and I imagined paddling quietly among golfers, a sudden gallery of canoeists creating shaky backswings as they attacked the fairways. We stopped to watch a pair of crows harassing a great horned owl.

The dipping of paddles kept us pleasantly warm. Some even enjoyed a light sweat. Everyone nipped at water bottles or jugs of coffee and tea.

We crossed a pair of dams, sidling easily across the steel structure at Winnetka Road and undergoing a full-blown portage at Beckwith Road.

This is where the Forest Preserve District would make a lot of friends by cutting a canoe chute through part of the useless dam. Two daredevils in kayaks showed how it would work, slipping through a gorge of boulders on the west side of the river. That's fine for kayaks, but not for canoes.

41

We had trouble just getting out of the water. Six-foot ice shelves stretched from both banks. There was no way to climb out without either tipping or plunging through thin ice.

Then Jim Hart and Amy Hobbs found a way. They made a big loop in the water and paddled like maniacs toward shore, skidding onto the ice, sliding clear to the bank. "Canoe-luge" did the trick. Alighting had become easy and safe.

But now we felt the cold. A front had darkened the sky, dropping temperatures into the low 20s. Idling around the portage, nibbling granola bars, became uncomfortable. Sweat chilled turtlenecks and fingers numbed from the chill. I couldn't get back into Vic's canoe fast enough, to feel the muscles moving again.

We were done in just two hours, hauling boats up the bank, tying things down, heading for hamburgers. One kid was blue with cold, but she had been a passenger and didn't have the luxury of paddling. She would have been much more comfortable had her folks let her paddle to keep warm.

"When Ralph Frese first suggested I paddle this stretch of river, I thought he was crazy," Hurtowy said. "I figured this was the Chicago River. I didn't want anything to do with an open sewer. But one year he coerced me and I saw how beautiful it was and how much more wonderful it could be. Two weeks later, I went to my first Cook County Clean Streams Committee meeting."

Hurtowy now is a mover and shaker along the Chicago and many other Illinois streams. He and a growing list of river fanatics are reclaiming the resources of our streams.

"We're still a small group," he said. "This area has 8 million people, but only 50 were out here using this resource today. People need to wake up and see what we have right here in Chicago."

I gave him a silly look. Idealism may be fine. But there were no mobs on this city river. Solitude dominated even the roar of Dempster Street.

So, why spoil the secret?

January 22, 1995

Nothing like a freezing, bouncy, fume-filled, noisy arctic ride

I know now what my next dream trip is to be. I'll ride a makeshift caboose behind the snarling roar of a giant D-6 Caterpillar. Wearing ear cups and breathing diesel fumes, I'll take a "Cat train" across frozen tundra at the whoopee speed of 4 m.p.h. Now, how's that for kicks?

My spine and kidneys will notice every ripple of the land and ice, but I won't mind. I'll bunk on a homemade pallet, hoping I'm not dumped onto the floor in the middle of the night. And I'll smile contentedly, because now and then I'll get to hop off, unload a snowmobile and take a spin up some ancient wilderness corridor, following cryptic piles of Inuit signal rocks called inukshuks. When possible, a guide and I will race 15 or 20 miles ahead of the "train" to an icy lake, chop some holes and try to catch enough trout for everyone's dinner before the Cat catches up.

I'll point my sled toward musk oxen and herding caribou, and if the moon is right and I can stray far enough from the noisy Cat, I might even hear the howl of an Arctic wolf. I'll spend a good deal of time off that Cat train, riding ridges, exploring abandoned Inuit camps, drinking in the lonely splendor of the Arctic and perhaps helping the native guides harvest a caribou or two for "camp meat," as the needs depend.

I'll do this on and off for six days, or however long it takes bearded, boisterous Keith Sharp to drag this sled train through the snowy Canadian wilderness to his remote Ferguson Bay Lodge a couple of hundred miles beyond the sparse Inuit settlement of Rankin Inlet.

Sound like fun? Well, you've got to like a little pain . . .

Until this dream came along, the only time I laid eyes on Rankin Inlet was from the scratched windows of a well-worn bush plane. The gray day made for a bleak sight of stark, blocky houses on the windswept shores of upper Hudson Bay.

We'd flown there from the old Northwest Territories trading post of Baker Lake, our eyes peeled for signs of musk oxen on the tundra. That and the caribou are about all the wildlife you can see from planes up there in winter. Now and then you may see a seemingly endless snowmobile track to nowhere. Now I'm hoping to make one.

We paused that time only a moment at the Rankin airstrip, and soon were off to the comparative bright lights of Churchill, well down the coast into Manitoba. I never dreamed I'd want to see Rankin Inlet again. But last week old Keith Sharp changed that. At a coffee table during the All-Canada Show at Pheasant Run, Sharp described the problem he has supplying his remote lodge on the storied Kazan River, once the stomping ground of legendary explorer Samuel Hearne.

There is only one way Sharp can haul fuel, food, tools and building materials to his lodge and outposts on land that becomes little more than mossy muck from spring through fall. And that is by hauling three or four loaded sledges behind his Cat during the milder April stage of winter, when the ground still is firm enough to support loads of, say, 40 tons.

Ever the entrepreneur-not to mention the devoted mayor of Rankin Inlet, population 800, give or take few hides drying on stretchers-Sharp wants to see if he can sell rides on that supply trip to Arctic fools like me.

"If you can put up with the noise and fumes, it probably would be fun," he said with a savage grin. I told him I'd think about it-and then began counting the days.

Sharp's contemplated "package" includes a first-day jaunt by dogsled from Rankin. "Oh, maybe 40 miles or so," he said. "Then you'll build an igloo and spend the night, and you'll hear the Cat coming in the morning."

Some wakeup, I said. That Cat'll shake apart any igloo I try to make. Sharp's eyes filled with mirth at the thought.

He said if I was nice he'd try to talk Lisa Oolooyuk into supplying her dogs. A 19-year-old half-French, half-Inuk beauty queen from Rankin, Lisa is the new regional tourism chief for the Territorial government. An ardent native traditionalist, she also runs some 30 dogs. And she cooks, Inuit-style.

"If you are really nice, Lisa will introduce you to some of her native specialties," Sharp said. This led Lisa into a litany of exotic dishes that even I have never tried-like caribou chitterlings (her favorite). "Just boil," she said.

"But when you are cleaning them, be sure that the liquid is either brown or whiteish," Keith interjected. "If it's yellow, there's too much acid in that part, so throw it away."

OK, I said, gloomily taking note.

He also said, if we're lucky, Lisa will have aged a walrus under rocks for at least a year. "It's very good," she said. "It sort of has a sour tang."

The real delight apparently comes if you have a walrus that has been aged all of two years, Keith said, his chin whiskers bobbing maniacally. "This is when it loses some of its texture. Some of it turns green. And there are bug tunnels honeycombed throughout, but don't worry, because the bugs have gone. Blue cheese is the closest thing I can compare it to. Good, strong blue cheese. A really strong blue cheese."

Lisa said not to forget paquti, a dip made by stuffing caribou or seal marrow jelly into a pouch made from the large intestine, then hung until the bag turns stiff and dry.

"You use it as a dip for frozen or dried caribou meat," Lisa said. "The caribou marrow comes out chunky, while the seal dip is liquid, and much more sour."

But you don't have to go to such extremes to blend with the natives, she said. "Everyone is eating frozen fish with soy sauce these days. It a very modern thing up there." I glumly nodded. That's sushi, Inuk style.

So goes life on the Cat train, a modern trip into an ancient culture. Snowmobiles and sled dogs. Igloos and cabooses. Diesel fumes and seal dip. Bring your own cigars.

November 30, 1994

Lake trout fishing close to home is about as good as it gets

You may think it just a tad nippy these days to brave three- to five-foot swells on Lake Michigan just to catch a fish. Then again, you may be one who would swim through ice cubes, if necessary, to nail the big, big lake trout that are available in Indiana's harbors.

For years, the fall laker run was a blood secret among the cognoscenti. Habitues like Jim Saric would sneak around for three or four weeks without telling even their closest buddies. Theirs was the unspeakable triumph of having a world-class fishery all to themselves. Well, human nature resists a code of silence. Sooner or later, mouths begin to flap. The trickling word eventually becomes a torrent of excited verbiage. Even so, pressure for these lakers remains negligible along the Indiana shore. Perhaps the fall is more for hunting than fishing. Then, a lot of people have stowed their boats for the winter. Even Saric, the editor of Muskie Hunter magazine, has begun to talk about it without thinking his best spots will be overrun.

Veteran lake watcher Lefty Frum says 12 to 20 boats a day now plow from Lefty's Coho Landing near Portage for the 1-mile crossing to Port of Indiana. Others ply Gary's Jeorse Park, surreptitiously trolling the boat-empty harbor, and still more test the rock walls near Michigan City. Nowadays, it's pretty hard for anyone not to find a laker. The big surprises can be some very large steelhead that hang around to gobble up those trout eggs, and some brown trout to eight pounds that lurk among the berths of ocean ships. And, if you really want your head turned, Frum says this is the time to catch humongous northern pike at Port of Indiana.

"They've gone as high as 18 to 19 pounds near the grainery," Frum reported. "Corn and wheat get spilled there and shoots grow in the water. The pike apparently love it. You can get 'em on June Bug spinners with frozen smelt. Or just on Dardevle spoons. They'll be there until March."

When I told Saric about the pike, a phenomenon of only the last couple of years, he shrugged and continued rigging his rods for lake trout. "It gets to be a passion," he apologized, tying small snaps to 17-pound test line on baitcasting rods. We'd be throwing crankbaits or jigging spoons-"although if you bothered to use live bait like golden roaches, you'd probably catch a fish with every cast. But then it would be too easy."

So what if I like it easy? Saric gave an evil grin. "It's too much trouble to look for live bait," he shrugged.

So we'd do it the hard way—Saric, Spence Petros and myself. We'd flash our sonars around the Port of Indiana until we found a school of swirling, spawning trout. Then we'd hit 'em in the heads with flashy lures in hopes of diverting them from nature's most compelling summons. Fat chance, I thought. Fat chance, indeed.

With three casts, Petros—editor of *Fishing Facts* magazine—decided the crankbaits were not going to work, so he switched to a half-ounce Luhr-Jensen jigging spoon. He soon had a nice 12-pounder. When he caught a second laker, I scrambled for the spoons, caught a bigger fish, and now Saric was pawing through the tackle box.

"Awright, you guys," he said. "I was just trying to be civil." He soon had a fine laker while weaving his trolling motor along the edge of a school that had to contain 100,000 fish. "You can tell where they are by the milkiness of the water," Saric noted.

By casting our spoons into the pods of fish, then jigging the spoons back in a series of fluttering drops, we caught perhaps 25–30 fish. None was smaller than eight pounds, some reached 16 and the average probably was 12. Saric has four or five obvious places where he routinely finds schools within the protected port. But he'll catch them on the outside, too, whenever the water is calm. "I'll be able to do this for two or three weeks," he said.

Petros noticed the lakers like to gang up on shelves or submerged ledges in corners and elsewhere, and said the trick is to stay just far enough from the fish to reach them with casts while not spooking them with a boat. He observed that whenever a certain boat parked directly above the fish, no one caught anything.

"If you play this right, it's incredible," he said. "People can go to Canada all their lives and never experience the kind of lake trout fishing we have here right now."

These, of course, were nothing like the benign lakers hauled from deep water by trollers in the heat of summer, when little else is happening on the lake. Too often, those are lethargic fish, effectively suffering "the bends" as they are dragged through the steep column of water. These shallow autumn fish—caught in 16 to 32 feet of water—are fighters who'll haul lines on half a dozen powerful runs.

"The thing is, we're just realizing this fall fishery is not simply related to Indiana," said Saric. "It starts farther north earlier, then works its way down as the water temperature changes. This year they probably were in Waukegan at Halloween. The reason they are here now is because this is the last of the warm water in the lake."

CHAPTER FOUR
LUNCHTIME

Tribune colleague Andy Bagnato remembers calling John one day with a problem: An opossum had taken up residence beneath Bagnato's porch, and he didn't know how to get rid of the pest.

Bagnato wanted the name of a trapping service. John gave him a recipe.

That's the way it was with John. He had an ironclad creed: If he killed something, he would eat it.

Fortunately, he also had an ironclad stomach. Over the years, John ate crow, quite literally; savored the reviled carp; sampled the lowly prairie dog. Mountain lions became gourmet fare in John's world, as did deer, bears and squirrels.

The Olympics? John saw them not only as the world's largest sporting events but also the world's largest buffet, providing such delicacies as asparagus cookies and eel jerky.

They also provided fodder for some of his most memorable columns.

October 23, 1991

Food for thought for 4th graders

Dear Mr. John Husar,
Our class, the 4th grade, was reading about prairie dogs. How could
you eat a prairie dog! . . . You would not like it if I turned you into a
hamburger. Don't do that again.
From a 9-year-old girl at Transfiguration School

To the students of Mary Dyer's 4th grade class at Transfiguration
School in Wauconda:

Thank you for your letters about the prairie dogs. I can see how you
were shocked to learn those cuddly creatures are good to eat.

You probably never thought of prairie dogs as food. Or as dangerous pests that ranchers want to eliminate. But little piglets and baby
chicks are just as cuddly. So are calves, which grow up to give us milk,
ice cream and hamburgers.

As long as we live in a meat-eating society, we will have to kill some
animals for the pantry.

And we'll always be killing pests. In cities, they can be anything
from stray dogs and cats to mosquitoes, houseflies and sewer rats. In
some of our forest preserves, pests include raccoons and deer. There
are just too many deer. They bother homeowners, ruin natural areas
and sometimes run onto the highways and cause terrible accidents.
Some must be removed or we will have worse problems.

People who live in the country have other pests: coyotes, field mice,
crows. In some places where people live close to wilderness, pests
include mountain lion, bear and even buffalo.

Here in Illinois, farmers think our big deer herds are kind of pesty.
They eat too much corn and soybeans. They wreck orchards and
Christmas tree farms. While we like our deer, we can't afford too

many, so we encourage hunters to kill and butcher them for their good meat, called venison. Hunters may take only so many deer each year. That helps wildlife managers thin the herds and keep them strong. New deer are born to replace the ones that were harvested. A balance exists. Hunters take the place of wolves and bears and mountain lions in Illinois.

For those of us born and raised in cities, the act of killing animals can be hard to imagine. No good person wishes cruelty on anything that lives. But human beings intend to control their environment. They want things a certain way. They boss the animals. They tolerate the ones that don't bother them, and they get rid of the others. Like it or not, that's our way. Animals are penned and slaughtered for food, poisoned as pests and hunted for both reasons.

I prefer to hunt my food, whenever possible. It's a better deal for me and the animals. They get to live freely and nobly. And from time to time, under very restrictive conditions, some of them are harvested and taken home and cooked. Most go on living in the wild.

You may think I'm kidding, but the tastiest meat comes from wild game. Well, I like pork and lamb, too. But my freezer at home contains a lot of food that most of you probably haven't tasted. Right now, my wife and I have neatly marked packages of venison, pheasant, quail, dove, duck, geese, bear and antelope. We also have salmon, bluegill, crappie, walleye and northern pike.

The fish we catch are animals, too, and they are just as important.

If you ever came to my house, that's what you'd get to eat. Maybe deer, maybe duck, maybe bluegills. You'd probably like it. Ask your dad or an uncle or a family friend who hunts to bring some wild game to your house someday. I'll bet your mothers would make something delicious.

One of my favorite foods is squirrel. That's right, those cuddly things that live in trees. Like prairie dogs, they are rodents. But most rodents are good to eat. When you think of it, their diets are cleaner than many pigs or chickens.

I like my squirrel "wet fried," which means breading the pieces and frying them in broth and wine. That's one way I cooked my prairie dogs. It's good for rabbit, too. In fact, wet frying was invented for rabbit meat, another delicious "cuddly" dish. If you want to know how rabbit tastes, look in the frozen meat section of a Dominick's or Jewel store. They carry excellent rabbit, although it's not as tasty as the rabbit that lives in the wild. The difference is the same with chickens. The pen-raised chicken you buy in stores just isn't as tasty as the chickens that live in a farmer's barnyard.

I know it's hard for city folk to think of food as having been alive. We never raise or kill the meat ourselves. Farmers and butchers do it for us, and we pay them for their services in the price. Country folk smile at our hangups, like the boy or girl who is asked by a mother to kill two or three chickens for Sunday dinner or the farmer who butchers a hog for the freezer.

When I went to Montana last month, it was not to harm the millions of prairie dogs in the West. It was not to poison them by the thousands so they wouldn't ruin a pasture. It was not to kill them and leave them lie, to be eaten by other wildlife. It was to see how good they taste. I hoped, if they tasted good, to convince ranchers to eat them and enjoy them instead of just try to get rid of them, even though no one really can get rid of all the prairie dogs in the West.

So in answer to your questions, yes, they tasted good. Not like squirrel. That surprised me. They were different, as sage-reared western deer tastes different from corn-raised Illinois deer. The next time I go West, I'm going to hunt prairie dogs again and bring a few home to my freezer. Some of my friends want to see how they taste.

All animals are cute. Some rub noses and worship their mothers. Some eat their brothers and sisters. They are animals, not people. But even animals that aren't food deserve our respect.

The same day I took those two prairie dogs, I met a rattlesnake on the side of a road. I admired the snake and thanked it for the courtesy of its warning. Then I wished it well and left.

JOHN HUSAR

April 5, 1992

The mane course: He takes a lion's share for his supper

I know, I know. You think this is getting out of hand.

Opossum, you could understand. Southerners have known it as a delicacy for years. Carp, too. A tasty fish, the victim of misguided hangups.

With fish liver, crow and prairie dog, we may have edged toward culinary outer space. People still can't believe we've found ways to cook 'em right.

And you should have seen the faces of the relatives when we presented tenderloin of black bear at Christmas.

Well, I'm even more convinced now that any kind of game has merits on the table. Especially since we solved the mystery of what to do with Ralph Cianciarulo's mountain lion.

"A cat?" sneered my editor. "You're going to write about eating a cat?"

Well . . . in fact, yes. I've even informed my trio of house cats the tables have been turned and they better know who's boss. No more yowling for food at 6 a.m. No more hissing at the dog. They now are only slightly more secure than those scrumptious neighborhood squirrels, which are protected by ordinance, unfortunately.

The mountain lion came into our kitchen as an experiment, my having stumbled across a little secret while hunting deer and antelope in Montana. It seems ranchers and guides who know about mountain lion never let that precious meat get away.

They're always glad to see a hunter take the head and hide for trophies, as hunters will. They make the hunter think they're glad he helped them eliminate a livestock predator. And they encourage him to leave the carcass as food for the dogs. They'll take care of it. No problem. Hah!

At a waterfowl dinner in central Illinois, a former Wyoming game warden confirmed how he and his cohorts would race to the check-in station whenever they would hear someone had downed a big cat. They would gang around, compliment the hunter, help him skin the critter. Hey, they would even get rid of the carcass for him. They got rid of it all right. At Sunday dinner.

After a meal at Montana's famous Road Kill Cafe last fall, a trapper-guide boasted of canning a year's supply of venison, antelope and, yes, mountain lion. And guess what his family devoured first?

Well, Chicago bowhunter Ralph Cianciarulo happened to be heading for Montana a few weeks ago to film a mountain lion hunting video.

"You know what I want," I mentioned before he left.

"Don't worry," he replied. "I'll make sure you get the meat."

Ralph's package came last week. A Montana butcher had processed, wrapped and frozen the 120-pound female into catly roasts, tenderloins and steaks, just like venison. Ralph said the locals were aghast.

"You mean you're gonna take it all home?" they moaned.

He grinned.

"They acted like I was making off with something that rightfully belonged to them. They couldn't believe someone in Chicago was going to eat it."

Well, the acid test came last Wednesday night. I phoned a few friends to announce we were breaking out the mountain lion and they were welcome to drop by the house for a taste. You never have seen people fumble so fast for flimsy excuses. Even Ralph had things to do.

"I wanted you to taste it first," he later confessed.

I'll admit I wasn't worried. I once had tasted tenderloin of African lion at a posh game dinner at Max McGraw Wildlife Foundation that also included fillet of camel. While the camel emerged something like a ham steak, the lion was an eye-popper. It had the milky texture of a pork roast–light, mild, richly flavored.

Our problem was a major lack of recipes for mountain lion. One book lamely recommended frying cubes of cougar meat in oil, which sounded like a waste of meat. Especially a meat that felt so tender we put away the pressure cooker.

Lacking any further guidance, one roast went into the oven antelope-style. That meant roasting a chunk of meat in bouillon with Worcestershire, soy, onion, garlic salt, sherry, mushrooms and a grated carrot.

Another roast was cubed for the same stew that worked so well with prairie dog, first a marinade of milk, garlic, onion salt, paprika, egg, Worcestershire and soy, then a Brunswickian compote of tomatoes, corn, lima beans, mushrooms, onion, basil, cayenne and red wine.

Next, thick cuts of tenderloin were hammered flat, seasoned, breaded and fried. A neighbor, Stan Kawinski, fried some without breading, so we really could taste the meat. He also contributed a splendid side dish of creamed onions and mushrooms. If you haven't noticed by now, we are big on mushrooms.

The verdict? That was left to a cousin, Brian Butkus. As the only teenager on hand, he was deemed most expendable and given the dubious honor of first bite.

Brian manfully forked in some stew.

"Excellent," he pronounced.

He was kind enough not to notice the stew meat turned out a little tough because we didn't cook it long enough.

But the tenderloins were out of this world, especially with a currant-based Cumberland sauce or the gooseberry chutney my wife brought from Scotland. And the roast? Well, the roast was a keeper. Nothing—not a shred—was left on the platter.

"It's hard to typify this flavor," neighbor Chuck Novotny mused, "because I've never tasted anything like this before."

We had anticipated something porky, or maybe a little like veal. But neither was right.

The roast happened to be somewhat overdone and fell apart at the slicing. The sharp chunks were unusual. Phyllis Kawinski, working on her second helping, finally made the connection.

"You're going to call me crazy, but I think it tastes like turkey," she said.

The faces around the table were thunderstruck. The chunks of white meat glistened in sauce like turkey a la king. We jammed down another bite in unison. The richness . . . the flavor . . . was of a lovely roasted turkey.

Ralph was stunned the next day.

"Hey, that's my favorite," he protested over the phone. "I'm leaving to turkey hunt in Georgia on Sunday night. And I gave it away. Damn! Now I have to go back and shoot another cougar again."

That's OK, he was told. We'll do the honors for him when he gets back. Just as long as the rest of this delicious cat stays safely in our freezer. At least until Easter. The family never will know.

JOHN HUSAR

August 14, 1996

Pursuit of fresh raspberries is one of summer's top picks

Here is some free advice: Never resume work after a month's hiatus while a spouse cooks raspberry jelly in the next room.

The aroma obliterates outside thoughts. All you can do is sneak into the kitchen to dip a spatula into the mixture and try to steal some licks without a measuring cup flying at your head.

Raspberries have been my healing balm after the logistical horrors of Atlanta. For those who pay no attention to what else goes into this sports section, I had joined a number of colleagues in the purgatorial quest for Olympic truth. Now it was time to get back to my real purpose in life—which at the moment involves a manic search of the countryside for plants abulge with peaking raspberries.

The rains and humidity have contributed to a bumper crop. I can't remember seeing so many huge and luscious berries. Some patches contain so much fruit you can stand in one spot for 10 minutes of rapid picking, raking handful after handful into the bucket that dangles from your wrist.

Time and worry evaporate. I call this the Zen of berry picking. The mind focuses totally upon the beatific gift of this beautiful and compelling fruit. On the nether side, a rising greed commands you to collect every berry in the patch, on the farm, in the neighborhood.

The quest becomes hypnotic. Just when you think you have stripped the mother of all berry clusters, a fluttering leaf reveals a twin hidden not 15 inches away. Your eyes spin and fingers flail as you are sucked deeper into the vortex, the need to control more and more berries.

Time indeed stands still. A mantra of repetitive song squeezes out ancillary thoughts. This week it was Ado Annie's inability to say no from "Oklahoma!"—a maddening refrain.

I fail to hear birds chirp or note the movement of the sun. I have been told of sprinkling rains, but I don't remember. Only dimly am I aware of my loyal dog underfoot, slurping fallen berries. Sometimes the mental fog is penetrated by a breeze, which refreshes the body and confuses some of the hundreds of disturbed, hungry mosquitoes swirling around, the price you pay for seeking this particular pot of gold.

I have come to grips with these mosquitoes. Bear hunters would understand. To hunt bear, you hunker near marshy lowlands amid clouds of whining mosquitoes, accepting them without a swat or the tiniest revealing movement. Ergo, I find my best berries in the sand prairies and woodland edges of northern Illinois, which always breed abundant mosquitoes. You can't escape them. Avoid mosquitoes and you'll miss the berries.

My face, neck, ears and the backs of my hands are swathed in repellent, along with hat, jeans jacket and thorn-resistant brush pants. The dog also has been sprayed with stuff from a pet shop, so she can gorge on berries without being eaten alive. The insects still corkscrew behind glasses, up sleeves and into ears. But when your hands are full of berries and hundreds more dangle before your eyes, you take another step into the thorny mess.

Each step jars awake another cloud of tiny-brained mosquitoes who groggily regard you as a steak dropped onto their plates. Just when they begin losing interest is when you need to take another step. The battle, of course, is worth the glory when the truck is laden with flats of fresh-picked, juice-bulging berries, enough for winter.

Now, I obviously do not pursue berries like most folks. I am not content to munch upon a handful while bringing home a pint for dessert. I pick berries with a holy passion, packing them into freezers so they'll be on my cereal in February and March. They are my connection to the munificence of nature. They bind me to my favorite haunts. It's the same as cooking self-killed venison, pheasant or ducks year-round. You remember where you have been. You see again the most special places.

This was one of the topics that kept a few of us together at the Olympics. As the host organization threatened to rend itself with mindless errors and awesome inefficiency, I gravitated to other displaced outdoor writers—guys from Detroit, New Orleans, Washington, Colorado. We would watch the Games while discussing crucial matters like ducks and squirrels. Other writers around us–unfortunate urban creatures—might twist their heads nervously at foreign tales of fly fishing in Michigan's streams, of waterfowling in Louisiana. The cleaning and cooking of delectable morsels repelled some of them.

Another topic was raspberries. We recognized the healing power of gathering fruits of the wild, be they berries, mushrooms, walnuts, rabbits, walleyes or birds on the wing. And we knew that, in a week or so, we all would be snugly in the bush in our home regions, sharing space with mosquitoes, happily restoring our lives with the life that was waiting for us out there.

February 14, 1998

Hold the octopus, but I'd like more asparagus cookies

Each day, at each Olympic event, it seems as if a plague of locusts has swarmed through the concession areas.

Usually, not a single asparagus cookie or tomato pretzel is left.

If nothing else, the Japanese taste for odd—if surprisingly delicious—victuals will leave an indelible impression upon Western Olympic visitors.

Those who are used to hot dogs and popcorn and maybe a plate of nachos at sports events are having their eyes peeled open to new culinary adventures.

The best substitutes the Japanese can offer are steaming bowls of noodles in wondrous broths, flavored with vegetables, beef or seafood.

I was at a ski race, slurping thick udon noodles with seafood tempura from an immense styrofoam bowl with some queasy American friends, when a pal began poking at tiny squares of a rubbery substance.

"What's this?" he wondered in a suspicious voice.

"Seafood," I replied, unwilling to wreck his lunch by revealing he had been eating octopus.

"I'll tell you this—Jerry Reinsdorf never would allow that," a fellow Chicagoan observed.

Breakfast at morning sports events often is the greatest challenge. Although Japanese hotel chefs gamely produce uncustomary variations of eggs—"sunny side up" means poached in frilly cupcake hold-ers—most public food stands and restaurants expect you to eat like the locals do.

That means rich bowls of miso soup, made from a bean paste, with paper-thin onion slices floating on the edges. Variously flavored rice—often with saffron or curry, and sometimes with smoked fish—is abundant. Soft rolls and marmalades. Juices and plenty of fresh fruit—although the Japanese propensity for refrigerating bananas often leaves them mushy.

Most coffees come in cans, dispensed from omnipresent vending machines. Most are laced with cream and sugar–sometimes with chocolate.

Many Americans have learned to paw through bins of cellophane-wrapped breads, if only to discover what might be inside.

One hefty roll at a concession stand contained a spicy tuna salad, loaded with cayenne, while another featured chocolate pudding.

A short French roll was sliced twice. One slice contained butter, the other chocolate pudding. It was amazingly tasty for breakfast with a can of coffee.

One wildly popular condiment is a banana cream roll. A round slab of banana bread is folded over a whole fresh banana and stuffed with whipped cream. No stand can keep it in stock for long.

Other popular pastries include churoki—bread soaked in maple syrup and fried—and a cinnamon roll stuffed with cherry jelly.

Sweets are abundant, from chocolate-dipped pretzels to taffies called "caramels." The most popular fruit-flavored taffy, as well as chewing gum, appears to be blueberry—or "bluebelly," as one phonetically challenged marketing department has labeled its product.

Almost every concessions area offers a variety of steamed Chinese-style stuffed buns in pork, curry and pizza flavors. These are well known in American Chinatowns on dim sum menus. The Japanese also are partial to tightly packed triangles of flavored rice wrapped in seaweed. It's a bit like nibbling a moist, sour, very loose granola bar.

French fries are available—from machines. Pull a paper cup from a holder, insert it beneath the food drop, put in a coin and you have a cupful of hot sliced potatoes—and not as greasy as you'd think.

Cookies abound—but none has chocolate chips. Yes, they're often made of materials like asparagus, tomato and even buckwheat noodle paste.

How good can asparagus cookies be? Well, even the finicky Bernie Lincicome helped himself to thirds.

One of the great touches occurs at the luge and bobsled course, where Bavarian music spices the atmosphere of essentially European sports.

Here Japanese concessionaires offer hot cans of fragrantly mulled wine, European-style, and now the locals have some discovery of their own.

The sight of five or six Japanese gingerly testing this foreign "glogg" emphasizes the universality of an Olympics.

So does the finger-sized morsels of squid available in every 7-Eleven convenience store.

"You just don't expect to see squid at a 7-Eleven when you're looking for pizza puffs," a bemused American said.

June 28, 1998

Here's the buzz: Walk in the woods yields sweet harvest

While this may come as heresy to some of my Slovak and Lithuanian relatives, there actually are more compelling reasons to visit the woods these days than mushrooms.

These are the gift of heaven itself—dark purple jewels the size of thumbnails. They're out there ripening by the jugful. I say this with a huge bowl of the morning's harvest beside me, slathered in yogurt.

Yes, this could be a monumental year for raspberries. Those heavy spring rains that delayed so many Midwestern farmers did a magnificent job on the wild fruit and nut crops.

We knew it might be good three weeks ago when the car was bombed with sodden mulberries from a tree along the driveway. These were the biggest, sweetest mulberries I'd seen in years.

Then a bike ride along some forest preserve trails yielded hints of raspberries to come. Clutches of berries abounded, just days from maturity.

Out near our cabin in northern Illinois, the raspberries came into their own this past week. The grandkids went crazy. They sliced through a couple of patches like threshing machines. They came away so stained with berry juice you'd have thought they had been painted for some weird rock concert.

I normally miss the height of raspberry season. I get a little busy chasing fish here and there. By the time I look around, most of these early plants are withered and barren. I always wonder if those patches ever hold good berries. This year I found out.

So I gear up for blackberry season in August, determined to gather enough for a winter's frozen supply and at least a dozen jars of jelly. The blackberries still are green. But judging by their bulging amplitude, they are preparing a bumper crop as well.

For once, though, I'm scoring big with raspberries—and not those little dried-out pebbles swiftly bleached by intense sunlight. These are blue-ribbon berries by county fair standards—immense, yielding cushions of goodness that roll, when touched, into your hands.

Of course, they don't come easily. I needed, as usual, a scout to lead me on a berry foray to a farm the other day, and the 9-year-old grandson luckily was available.

He explained to me there always is a price to pay for harvesting good things from the wild. And what might be a toll for raspberries?

"Thorns," he said. "You stick your arms through bunches of thorns."

That made sense. I have walked into country cafes in blackberry season looking as if I'd been in a cat fight, with blood-caked scratches on arms and forehead. In the realm of berries, I do get carried away. Of course, in those cafes people are tolerant. Everyone knows what you've been doing.

"And mosquitoes," the boy piped. "Don't forget the mosquitoes."

It is not within my power to forget mosquitoes. I am the kind of guy who climbs out of bed in the middle of the night to chase a single whining mosquito through the house.

Unfortunately, mosquitoes and berries go hand-in-hand, and that is something we berry people have to deal with. Now and then the berry gods will plant a patch on the windward edge of an open field and we will be spared, because mosquitoes are notoriously poor flyers in a breeze. That's why we camp on the windy point of a lake.

But catch them in a tight, muggy, airless corner of some small woody corridor or field and you offer your body to be eaten alive.

My scout thankfully found a nice patch where the bugs weren't too bad and, in 20 minutes, we picked well over half a quart. Then we drove around the farm to mark other patches, where I'd return on another day, swaddled in hooded jacket with neck scarf and head net, ready for serious business.

We were looking for heavy clusters of three-to-seven ripe berries on every plant, enough to funnel through a palm and straight into a bucket hanging from a wrist. When we rolled by an irresistible clutch in the back corner of a little field, I stopped the truck. And we paid the price.

I could hear an ominous hum of mosquitoes through the window, yet still I got out. The last time I heard that sound was in a tree stand on a bear hunt in Manitoba near a swampy pile of refuse. All you heard all day was the high whine of millions of mosquitoes, sort of like those old radio broadcasts of the Indy 500 with a constant whine of engines in the background. You sat through this protected by a nylon rain suit covered by a bug jacket and cans of spray and tried not to go nuts.

"Stay inside," I told the boy. "I just want to check these out." In seconds, though, he was beside me, arms flapping, eyes ablaze with horror.

"There are millions of them in the truck," he wailed. His head swerved and his voice rose. "And there are billions of them right here."

I had collected maybe 30 berries, but mosquitoes already were in my mouth and up my nose.

"I think we'd better go," I said, and the boy nearly burned a path back to the truck.

On the way to town, he cradled our combined bucket of raspberries in his lap, soon to savor the ultimate of rewards.

"I think there are a lot of prices you have to pay for raspberries," he intoned. "Mosquitoes . . . heat . . . humidity . . . thorns . . . and sunburn."

That, I told him, was about it. Fortunately no cloudbursts had completed the cycle.

We came to a roadside ice-cream stand in town and ordered a couple of tubs of vanilla, then packed in as many berries as the cups would hold. We squished them in by the scores, one for each mosquito, maybe half a pint apiece.

Then we sat by the railroad and waited for the explosive power of the 4:51 p.m. streamliner to ram through from Chicago.

"This has to be as good as it gets," said the boy, mimicking a TV commercial. He held up a spoonful of ice cream with 20 or 30 berries clinging to the mess. The cup swirled with a melting, purple, sticky, incredibly wonderful nectar.

I nearly made the mistake of suggesting there might be other fine experiences ahead in life, but managed to shut up in time. On this day, certainly, the kid had to be right.

JOHN HUSAR

February 7, 1999

Taking a shot at eating crow

Sue Fisher has a dangerous spirit that just might get her in trouble with the family.

When I asked if she wanted some freshly filleted crow breast, she gamely burbled, "Sure!"

Then she caught a cloudy glance from her hubby. Like most lawyers, Alan Fisher was not about to nibble any crow. Lawyers think it's bad form to eat crow.

I gave Sue a chance to reconsider: "So will you cook it? Will you try it?"

She thought a moment, then shook her head. Enthusiasm had vaporized. "I guess not," she said.

Well, I had to be sure. I was not about to waste any good, fresh crow meat on folks who were afraid at least to try it. Besides, I needed the meat for a cooking demonstration I'll be doing with Bill Cullerton Sr. and my wife, Louise, at the Sportsmen's Show of Chicago later this month.

Last year we sprung a compote of squirrel, rabbit and pheasant on an unsuspecting audience at the McCormick Place extravaganza. This year they'll eat crow, thanks to Alan and his brothers, Eric and Jeff Fisher.

Eric, a fellow outdoors writer who publishes the weekly Wilmington Free Press in Will County, had phoned the other day to see if I wanted to go crow hunting.

"The thing is, we'll have to blindfold you in the car," he needled. "This is too good a hunting place to share with a bunch of your readers."

I swore myself to secrecy and we arranged to meet near St. Charles. Eric, Jeff and I then went to Alan's house, which is only 10 minutes from "crow central," as far as the Fishers are concerned.

Alan explained he found this spot—a large suburban cornfield with all kinds of woody borders—three years ago.

"I was sitting at a stoplight when all these crows streamed overhead," he said. "Three hundred must have passed by in 2 minutes."

Alan had to see where those crows were going, so he followed them to this farm on the edge of town. It held everything a crow needs–hundreds of acres of picked grain, highways for carnage, water, a nearby dump, plenty of roosting trees.

Alan got permission from the farmer and now visits this spot maybe once a week during the split crow season that ends on March 1. He figures any more frequency might burn it out.

Not that the Fishers are obtrusive. Our little wooded point last Sunday overhung two leaf-camouflaged pop-up blinds. Thirty crow decoys were spread in the cornfield among the melting snow. Our pieces de resistance, however, were a pair of electronic callers, amplified tape players that sound as if a couple dozen crows are feasting. One tape sounds as though all these crows are having a fight. These are irresistible come-ons not only to crows, but flocks of pigeons, ducks and at least three curious geese. Up close, the noise resembled a beachful of screaming kids.

Crows absolutely have to take a peek. And while many wary ones do so from a safe distance, a goodly number wander into shotgun range.

That doesn't mean you'll hit them. Crows are stunt pilots, capable of the most amazing evasive aerobatics. Hunters who think doves are hard to hit might be ashamed to tally their scores against crows—even with heavy-duty 12-gauge, high-brass No. 6 shot.

"Most people misjudge them at first," Alan said. "We've had guys out who were pretty good shooters and it took them maybe 15 or 18 shots to bring down their first crow."

I can relate to that. Swaddled in a bulky winter coat, I had trouble mounting my gun at first. All my initial shots seemed high.

Not that these crows were cooperating. Most came in singles, with the biggest flock perhaps seven.

The Fishers were disappointed. They are used to fast and furious shooting into swirling flocks of 20 or more.

"Our best day was 72 birds by six guys in 3 hours," Alan noted. "One time I came out with Dick Shrader and we got 20 birds in 20 shots. But he is a wonderful shooter."

Maybe the day was too nice. Too soft and warm and placid. I spent a lot of time engulfed by the pastels of thick cloud formations as backdrops for distant strings of geese and ducks.

The best crow flights occur late in the day as they stream toward their roosts. But you have to be lucky or clairvoyant to pick the route they'll take.

In our case, we missed a lot and hit a few and were able to retrieve five birds. Eric and I breasted the crows beneath a tree. It was a start for the McCormick show's cooking school. Eric said he'll deliver more meat if he goes back. He hates the thought of anyone going hungry.

Here's how we'll cook 'em, in the manner of a nifty woodcock recipe in Geraldine Stendler's "Game Cookbook":

In a large skillet, we'll make a roux from 2 tablespoons of butter and 2 of flour. After tenderizing the crow breasts and scoring them with a sharp knife, we'll add them to the pot and coat them with the roux. Season with black pepper, pour on enough game stock to halfway cover the meat and splash on a tablespoon of vinegar.

Simmer until tender, then stir in a binding of an egg yolk, 2 tablespoons of sour cream, and 2 teaspoons each of cornstarch and lemon juice. Stir until gravy thickens, then blend in a tablespoon of capers, a splash of wine and a sprinkle of dried tarragon.

Believe me, this is top-drawer eating. Of course, it'll work for any other kind of flavorful game such as teal.

JOHN HUSAR

May 25, 1988

What's cooking?
Just about everything

I've always been an egg eater, any way you can name. Three over easy with country ham. Umm.

Scrambled with sauteed onions and green peppers and packed with mushrooms. Double-umm.

Chinese-style—fluffy and loaded with fresh shrimp.

And now I'll get to eat 'em thousands at a time. Now, anyway, that the perch are coming in.

I'd never tried fish eggs until Spence Petros took me to his house to clean a mess of perch.

"Oh boy," he said, exposing a pair of bulging egg sacs. "These are going to be tasty."

I gave him a curious look and he went on to explain the delicacy of well-prepared perch eggs.

When I suggested that he do more than explain, Spence performed a culinary miracle that since has led me toward a lot of other kitchen adventures.

As I watched, Spence slit the eggs free from a dozen little sacs, rolled them in Italian-seasoned bread crumbs and gently fried them in peanut oil. He then doused them with a sauce made of melted butter and lemon juice.

My first forkful was tentative. Then, heaven.

I've since tried perch eggs several ways, branching to the eggs of walleyes, crappies, any fish that I think palatable.

My personal contribution is a frittata variation. Mix a batch of clean, fresh fish eggs with a regular hen's egg or two. Add a splash of milk if you'd like to make it lighter. Mix in some chopped veggies, especially mushrooms, sautéed if you don't want them crisp. Don't forget the salt and pepper. I like lots of pepper. Fry in butter.

Bliss.

It sort of reminds me of a shrimp omelet.

All this came to mind when I read a recent *New York Times* story about an East Coast herring run. The writer recommended sautéing the herring eggs in garlic and oregano or using them as pizza toppings.

Caviar can be made by straining eggs through a large enough mesh to let individual eggs pass through. Rinse several times with cold water, salt to taste, drain and refrigerate.

Well, I figure, if that works with herring, it certainly should for perch.

I've gotten very choosy about what game parts I'll throw away. Livers, for example. I've always been a patsy for chicken livers wrapped in bacon and fried in pork fat.

Then on a trip to the Arctic, I tried that storied Inuit delicacy: raw seal liver.

I'd already learned to enjoy raw meats such as sushi and steak tartare, so the seal liver was nothing more than a pleasant surprise.

I brought some home and cooked it rare, like veal liver, and found its flavor lovely and delicate, with just a hint of the sea.

Well, I figured, if seal liver is so good, why can't regular fish liver be the same?

And so I tried the liver of walleyes and bass, cooking them just as chicken livers, but liking them even more. I now keep a little baggie of frozen livers in my freezer and add to them whenever I'm cleaning unpolluted fish. When I have enough, I cook them for company as hors d'oeuvres, never letting on what they are until they've been devoured.

I do the same with pheasant, partridge, ducks, geese and quail— collecting livers, hearts and gizzards until I have enough to bread lightly and deep fry. Believe me, they are wonderful. Skip the gizzards in waterfowl on the chance that they might be carrying the remnants of a lead pellet.

71

I realize that some of you are wrinkling your noses, but none of this should seem improbable if you consider the culinary delights of many peoples. Right now in Chicago, many Chinatown restaurants will serve you a nice appetizer of braised duck feet. Poles and Slovaks make homemade soups with duck blood and floating rooster heads. Lithuanians wolf down pickled pig's feet. Greektown restaurants offer platters of cracked-open lamb's heads.

Mexican grocers display whole hog's heads. Chitterlings are on sale throughout the city by the 10-pound tub. Japanese sushi bars vie for fresh, raw sea urchins. Never ask what goes into many sausages. Don't forget the guy in Wisconsin who sells baluts—chewy, half-developed duck embryos—to yuppie Asian restaurants.

So don't you question a cupful of fish eggs or livers.

There is one thing I haven't tried, and I've thought about it often, being one who enjoys a nibble of beef tongue now and then.

If tongue is tongue and liver is liver and hearts are hearts no matter whether fish, veal or fowl, what about all those nice, chunky bass tongues wiggling down there when you hold the mouth open to remove the hook?

I realize it is the practice of many sportsmen to release all bass, even though that isn't always necessary, or even wise from a few management perspectives. I toss 'em back to please my companions, more than anything else.

I do like to eat bass, but I rarely get to do so because of this convention. But the next time I'm with some folks who happen to kill a bass, I plan on doing a little sampling of my own.

How about sautéed, sliced bass tongue with a delicate wine sauce? Or maybe smoked, sliced thin and served on toothpicks with a spicy dip?

Anyway, don't throw away those perch eggs. You know better now.

CHAPTER FIVE
SIESTA

The scene could be the magnificent splendor of the Grand Canyon or a small stream cutting through bedrock just off a busy interstate highway. It could be sitting in a blind marveling at flocks of ducks overhead or sleeping in a tent.

It didn't make any difference. John found discoveries to be made and adventures to experience in places everyone else took for granted.

His writing made us pay attention to the great outdoors in ways we often overlooked and should be concerned about conserving. He could even turn the simplest overnight outing into something worth savoring for a lifetime.

JOHN HUSAR

May 22, 1988

Grandeur unfolds on river walks

Sometimes I just like to take a walk down a river.

If the water's right, I won't bother with boots or waders. An old pair of sneakers and shorts will do.

I'll start from a rural bridge in the "four corners" of Iowa, Wisconsin, Minnesota and Illinois and slosh as far as I can. In summer, when the water's lowest, you can make some goodly distances.

There are dozens of accessible streams in this arguably most beautiful part of the Midwest, where the glaciers refused to plane the hills and bluffs into cornfields.

For 300 miles on either side of the Mississippi River, a panoramic grandeur unfolds that is hard to explain to folks who've never been there and can't believe such wonders exist.

You drive, of course, to savor the overlooks and valley views and the sweet little fishing and boating villages tucked beside some of our nation's more biologically fertile backwaters. There are islands that you can reach, houseboats to rent, piers to fish, sanctuaries of all types. And, besides, there are plenty of rivers to walk.

Just try to count the big and little streams that reach the Mississippi between Savanna, Ill., and Winona, Minn.

And, if you mosey 30 miles inland either way among the twisting, climbing, diving country roads to nowhere—in their interlocked way, to everywhere—you will find another world of canoe trails, trout streams, bike paths and picnic spots that belong in the pages of photographic essays for coffee-table daydreams and fantasies.

I am always searching for another vista, another grasp of nature's splendor. But every time I return to these lovely and remote "four corners" of the Midwest, I wonder why I travel any farther.

Here are all the fishing and hunting that can fill a day, and more hidden pathways than one could hope to find. The Mississippi itself offers constant variety, including broad, lake-like bulges called Pepin and Onalaska.

Although some of those backwaters will be hard to cover by boat this summer—given another spring of low waters—they hold exquisite promise for future seasons. The low water already is sprouting huge growths of aquatic plants that will shield the products of another fruitful spawn, promising an even more tremendous fishery in years to come. The local duck hatch has been one of the best in years.

This is a place, especially in winter, to see an eagle grasp a thermal to scan the water for the silvery clue of a meal. Here thrives the secretive river otter, sliding purposefully down a bank at the break of dawn.

Unless you're in a boat, there are two best ways to see this part of the Mississippi in the fall—up Minnesota Hwy. 61 and back down Wisconsin Hwy. 35 north of La Crosse. The sunlight and terrain provide entirely different slants and colors.

Heading one way, the opposing hillsides tend toward pinks and reds among the greens. Coming back, the world swims in pinks and yellows, as sunnier slopes turn a week ahead of the others.

Then again, if shadier sides are scorched by an early frost, they may forge subtle tones of lavender. Each valley offers its own sense of color and grandeur, particularly where chokers of wild grapevine clasp the stately trees in garlands of pinks and roses.

The spring, too, has its moments as tender leaves emerge in 14 shades of green and yellow-green until they blend into the uniform of summer.

Each town along the river seems to have its festival and mansions that offer bed-and-breakfast. Be sure to catch the state-run aquarium at Guttenberg, Iowa, full of native river species, including a 20-pound sturgeon, that remnant of prehistoric times. Knowing pilgrims rarely pass the Eagle Valley refuge at Glenhaven, Wis. Elk, buffalo and other wildlife prowl Clayton County's Osborne Center preserve on the Turkey River at Elkader, Iowa. Some splendid hiking can be found at Effigy Mounds National Monument across the river from Prairie du Chien, Wis., at Marquette, Iowa.

Fully 80 percent of the Class I and II trout streams in Wisconsin, Iowa and Minnesota are publicly accessible, but county maps are vital and landowner permission to reach the streams is a must. Good maps are available from most county extension agents.

Houseboats can be found at many spots, including Winona, Minn., La Crosse, Wis., and Lansing and McGregor, Iowa. Decent and productive fishing floats are maintained for the public below dams at Lynxville and Genoa, Wis., and Dresbach, Minn. Free advice is available in every local bait shop.

Don't overlook local gun shops and hunter supply stores for tips on finding views of wildlife.

And if you really want to get away, take the time for an unforgettable walk on a shallow stream.

JOHN HUSAR

September 29, 1985

Country roads can turn a trip into an adventure

I'll never forget the sight of that one man running across an autumn field with his dog.

I was on a country highway and coasted to the side and watched, awed by that man's sense of freedom.

Why, he could run wherever he pleased. He could run side streets and country lanes, fields and woods. For all I knew, he could run the mountains and the beaches until he became a tiny dot on the horizon.

He probably could run farther than I could walk. He could reach places I couldn't. So I followed eventually, seeking that freedom to slip through neighborhoods and scenery, to know the jogger's intimacy with a world that sedentary bodies refuse to travel.

Whenever possible, I now do the same thing with my car.

I travel the interstates, hurrying from one outdoor adventure to another. But whenever I can, I try to capture small adventures in between.

That means getting off the blasted expressways.

How many times have you stared across the bleak expanse of manicured highway shoulders toward the remote quarters of hidden farmsteads and wondered how a drive through the country could be so barren and ugly?

Well, get off and find the opposite.

I still use the interstates to hurry to appointments. But whenever possible, I give myself an extra hour or so of daylight on the return trip. I leave the rat race for a slower pace on country roads.

Author William Least Heat Moon had the idea when he fled some personal problems along the back roads of America, unexpectedly gathering the wondrous impressions that led to his best-selling "Blue Highways."

But I am talking smaller roads than numbered highways on a map. I am extolling roads that may not appear on state maps: two-lane blacktops and paved farm-to-market roads.

Oh, numbered highways can be fine if they are relatively free of trucks. You'll find the best ones paralleling major expressways, such as U.S. Hwy. 30 to Clinton, Iowa, or U.S. Hwy. 45 and Ill. Hwy. 37 between Arcola, Ill., and southern Illinois. You can speed or loaf through charming countryside, dally through pretty towns, taste the surprises, sniff the sweet air, swap the waves and smiles.

My wife and I once drove 350 miles to Des Moines from Chicago, avoiding the blur and fumes of Interstate Highway 80. We took 2 days on U.S. Hwy. 6. We read every historical marker, saw every park, had a cup of coffee in nearly every town. We got as far as Princeton, Ill., the first night, catching a sunset as a high-speed freight train leaned through a sharp bend near the railroad depot. The next night was in

Iowa City, where we found an outdoor concert. We still talk about that trip.

Where no expressways draw the heavy traffic, try state roads that penetrate the country served by federal highways. These are smaller and freer of bullying trucks. And then there are the unmarked county highways that link towns that no one on the expressways ever sees.

After a weekend of teal hunting last month in Downstate Illinois, I felt my way toward Chicago on roads like these and found things that still leave me flushed with wonder.

I left Havana on an unmarked highway that wound northeasterly along the Illinois River. When it ended, I found another, and another, always moving north or east. In two hours I was in Gridley, at a little dairy where I bought some homemade cheese.

I ran into one dead end at a pretty little fishing lake in McLean County. A beautiful road had led, for miles without signs, directly to a boat ramp. I lost the miles, but now have another place for bass.

Three times I crossed the Mackinaw River and three times I saw inviting holes in sandy flats and cursed myself for leaving my rod at home. That won't happen again.

I usually keep a pair of sneakers or waders in the trunk; this time I had both, and once I took a walk upstream and watched the fish scurry ahead.

Fishing can be wonderful at country bridge abutments, or upstream around a bend. Those who use the back roads now and then grant themselves half an hour to wet a line and engrave a pleasant scene.

I have never been disappointed on the back roads, especially since I took up hunting.

People keep telling me how hard it is to find a place to hunt, and that is so, especially for those who seek a place at the last moment. Farmers stare in suspicion at strangers and shake their heads.

But if you stop along a country road to admire a man's woodlot or fencerow on a summer's break or in the early fall, he just may find it hard to turn you down. Especially if you offer to help him set up for hunting. Or offer to share the bag. Or promise to bring him a package of goodies from the city.

I know backroads travelers who never lack a place to hunt.

There are counties in southwestern Wisconsin where a fisherman can visit eight good trout streams on a single blacktop. And stop for lunch in a café with farm-fresh eggs.

I hardly ever travel the Borman Expressway around Lake Michigan in northwest Indiana without detouring toward the Port of Indiana and poking through the dunes along U.S. Hwy. 12 as far as Michigan City. It costs an extra 20 minutes, but it heals a lot of stress.

The best advice to see the most is to give yourself a little time—and, like the jogger, much more freedom.

JOHN HUSAR

August 24, 1994

"Grand" weekend for fishing—and passing the torch

We'd run out of worms at last, which meant the grandkids probably wouldn't feel any more tugs from smallmouth bass, but they didn"t know it.

Four-year-old Mikey disgorged the tangled array of plastic grubs, tails, craws and creatures that he'd stuffed into his pockets while rifling my bait box for treasures. He laid them in the sand beside the railing of a country bridge. He picked out the biggest, fattest, mean-est-looking crawfish and had his dad impale it on a hook. Then he cast the thing loudly into the creek.

Jon, the 5-year-old, was much more sophisticated. He selected a nice green tail for his green Roadrunner jig, took careful aim and zinged it toward a rocky outcropping on the far side of the stream. It smacked the water a foot from the bank, and he swam it back toward the bridge.

His dad and I looked at each other. Either of us would take a cast like that.

Suddenly, the rod bent and the boy's eyes nearly exploded. "I got one!" he shrieked. But as hard as he reeled, he couldn't make it move.

He handed me the rod and I felt the snag. "I think you have a rockfish," I kidded, but he was taking this seriously.

"A rockfish!" he bellowed as I tried to free his hook. "What does a rockfish look like?"

Instead of a rock, up came a submerged branch. "I guess you have a treefish," I said, still trying to be light.

The kid shot a withering glance at the perceived sarcasm. I wanted to say you live and learn, but I wisely said nothing.

The boys cast their improvised lures for half an hour—just playing with rods and reels and lures in a stream. Practicing without knowing it. Learning the imperatives of nosing miscast bait through overhangs without getting the hooks caught. At last we sidetracked them onto what we implied might be a hidden path to a secret Indian village somewhere over the rocks.

They prowled for a while, but there were too many choices, as befit state park paths. We never did find the Indians, but we did gather a handful of juniper berries from a windblown spray. When the boys heard that junipers are good spices for wild bird dishes, they collected some for Grandma.

Naturally, she wanted to know if they'd caught any fish, and right away I could see these kids were chips off the old block. "Oh, lots!" young Jon assured her. "Ten at least!"

Well, maybe it felt like 10, but actually we caught and released four smallmouth bass. That, when you think of it, isn't bad for a couple of hours on a country bridge with goofy rigs and a can of nightcrawlers.

Granted, I normally take on stream smallies with crankbaits or plastic grubs and metal spinners, but youngsters need an advantage. You can spend all day trying to tempt smallies with artificial baits. To be sure of catching some, especially when the protagonists are 5 and 4, I know of nothing better than a wad of fat crawlers. At least they'll feel fish, if any are around.

The boys wanted to know if these worms were big enough, as Mikey palmed a squirming 5-incher. Of course, the smallies thought they were fine.

While it's sort of hard for rank toddlers to make classic bait presentations in a flowing stream, they easily can get the hang of letting current carry their worms into the shadow of a bridge. If the bait happens to be near the bottom, and if it doesn't get snagged, they'll soon feel the rat-tat-tat of hungry fish.

That was the ultimate lesson for this day. They learned to feel an attack upon their hooks, and they gained whatever wisdom comes from missing a lot of fish. Good hooksets will come later. They did reel in the fish their dad caught, and that was as good as catching them. Well, nearly. At least until next time.

For me, it was the epitome of summer vacation. Hunkered on a remote country bridge with grandsons and a cherished son-in-law. Playing in an arena of summer wildflowers and teeming birdsong. Watching rods jiggle to the beat of smallmouth bass from a sparkling creek not far from the city.

This stream, like dozens in the upper third of Illinois, holds impressive numbers of smallmouth, rock bass, catfish, some largemouth, an assortment of carp and even toothy northern pike. You can wade most of these creeks, especially on public lands. But if the youngsters are small, all you really need is a bridge where a decent channel meets the shadows. Don't expect a lot of trophies. There at least will be fish if the water is good. Where are these spots? Check a map. There must be thousands of bridge spots like this in Illinois.

That was an especially memorable weekend. My city grandkids finally learned the difference between corn and soybeans. We pulled an ear of corn from a stalk and munched on the leathery sweetness. We found a wild plum tree and filled a coffee mug with tart, luscious fruit.

When Grandma took out the kids that night to wish upon a star, the 5-year-old scrunched his face and said he wanted to be a grownup with his own family and his own farm.

Later on, his dad and I sat outside for a couple of hours, savoring cigars and beer, serenaded by whippoorwills beneath a silvery moon, musing on families and farms. So this is how it feels to pass a torch.

JOHN HUSAR

May 13, 1998

Grown men heed the call of a baby goose in need

We all know passionate anglers who absolutely refuse to eat or even sip water when the fishing's on. They won't take time to gnaw on an apple. Not in 10 solid hours.

Spence Petros and I once found ourselves fishing for northern pike amidst a Canadian forest fire. Water planes bombed smoking trees not 200 yards from us. All we did was snap a couple of photos and cast a little deeper into the weeds.

The pilots looked in our faces as they pulled away, making screwball signs at their ears.

But show us a baby duck or deer or bird in trouble, and that is something else.

A bunch of us on Lake Michigan nearly were pecked to death by an angry gull we were trying to extricate from a fishing net. A pal and I once spent 20 harrowing minutes removing a muskie bait from an equally ticked 55-pound beaver on Lake of the Woods in

Canada. At one point, it was us or the beaver—and the beaver was winning.

So it went last week with George Liddle Jr. and Dan Keith from Midwest Outdoors TV on our bass excursion in the Chicago River.

I can't remember if it was George or Dan who first spotted the baby goose peering from the tall, steel-sided bank of a barge slip. But we all saw the cat at once—a black-and-white feral feline with yellow eyes fixed upon this week-old bundle of fluff fresh from the nest. The gosling had been chased onto a narrow ledge and now literally was peeping for its life.

"We have to rescue that goose," Keith declared.

"As if there aren't enough geese in this city," Liddle replied.

Keith launched into a speech about how geese can kidnap goslings from other clutches and that a pair of nesting, mature geese don't care whose kids they ultimately raise.

"OK, OK," Liddle said, gingerly guiding the boat toward shore with his electric trolling motor.

Then we saw a steel ladder hooked to the wall, allowing dockworkers to board barges. The ladder seemed extremely rickety—especially to guys on the large end such as Keith and myself.

"I don't care, we have to climb it," Keith said.

"What do you mean, we'?" Liddle grumbled, sliding the ladder closer to the goose.

He inched up, rung by rung, and scooped the goose. He handed it to me. I petted it and passed it to Keith in the rear of the boat.

"You know, I think we need a whole bunch of federal migratory waterfowl handling permits to do what we just did," I murmured uncomfortably.

We tooled around a couple of points, seeking a likely spot to leave the goose. By then, Keith had it nestled within his cap and was feeding it aquatic plants. That triggered a healthy biological function.

"What a choice," Keith grumbled. "I either wear a soiled cap or wash it in the Chicago River."

Wash it he did, and the goose was pleased.

It was so content that when we placed it on shore where it could be found by other geese, it promptly dove 10 feet into the water and swam madly after our boat. We cut the engine to let it catch up and it swam right into Keith's hat.

"He trusts you," Liddle said. "He thinks you're his mother."

Soon we found two nesting clutches of Canada geese on a fenced bank near Ashland Avenue. When the gosling was deposited behind the fence, a mated pair of mature geese sauntered over to inspect the newcomer. We last saw the little goose trailing his new parents.

While we caught more bass after that, the trip had climaxed. Nothing else came close to the allure of handling that fuzzy little goose.

That's what this outdoor stuff really is all about, I suppose—the wonder of discovery, the unexpected encounters with wildlife and nature's hidden world.

The fishing was superb. We caught more than 30 largemouth bass in the formerly polluted Chicago River within three hours. We would have caught more but for the 20 minutes spent coddling that baby goose.

But only a fool would have traded those 20 minutes for five more bass.

We'll always catch more bass. It's just not every day that you get hooked by a goose.

February 28, 1999

In this hunting family, she never had a chance

We were in the field on a golden false spring afternoon, my son-in-law Kevin, the three grandkids, our two dogs and me.

The dogs needed a stretch, so they were free to raise any of the club's gamebirds they might find.

Not that they would be all that lucky. Jenna, Kevin's boisterous Labrador puppy, was so charged by the idea of hunting that she took it upon herself to make a grand sweep through the smaller front field, trailed by my middle-aged Java, who was not about to miss any action.

"Well, that was quick," I mused when the happy dogs bounded back. "No birds there unless they have nerves of steel or are hard of hearing."

As we tried the next field, I thought of how the fates conspired against my sweet daughter, Kathi.

A product of the urban Southwest Side, she was raised with little exposure to country ways. By the time she finished college and was slipping a net around Kevin, she had come to regard hunting like most of the uninitiated—as something barbaric and coarse.

She not only never would hunt, but she would take a pass on the bounty from nature's pantry. Meat from a grocery was OK; meat that her father brought home from his own toil was anathema.

And then the man she married turned out to be a hunter. Poor long-suffering Kathi. At least she would protect her children from barbarianism and coarseness. Or so she thought.

Grandpa got his hooks into them with one simple gesture. On a day the family was coming to a picnic at Turkey Trot Rod & Gun Club, I planted just one pheasant in a thick row of corn and milo not far from the clubhouse.

When we later were outside admiring the scenery, I asked the kids if they would like to see how Java hunts. They, of course, said yes. We walked to the edge of the field and I asked Java to heel and sit. Then I pointed to the corn and said the magic words: "Java, find the bird."

The Lab was gone in a flash, plunging into thick vegetation. She picked up a scent trail and worked like a champion. By the time Java got abreast of us, the brilliantly plumed cock pheasant had been harried enough. It took to the air in a roar of beating wings and spun over the field.

Neither Kathi nor those breathless kids ever had seen a big, beautiful bird rise like that.

Java still was young enough to lose her head in the excitement. She watched it land in the middle of the field and broke after the pheasant. She chased it down, put it into the air again, then followed it toward some trees in the far corner of the field, far from us. And then Java disappeared into the woods.

We waited with increasing nervousness. One minute. Two minutes. Still no Java. I called once, hoping she hadn't crossed the road onto another farm.

Then a black blur emerged from the woods. Java pounded toward us through strips of tall grass as high as a man. One of the children noticed something in her mouth.

"It's a bird!" shouted Jon, the eldest, who was 6 at the time. "Java's got the bird!"

Indeed, a thoroughly confused pheasant rode unharmed in Java's gentle jaws, head up, peering around. Java brought it right to me and placed it in my hands.

Dear sweet Kathi had just lost the battle.

From then on, her kids hungered to return to the club, to plunge into gorgeous fields rife with mysteries. They didn't care if they would spook a pheasant or a meadowlark, a deer or a kangaroo mouse. They just had to be there, immersed in nature's gifts.

Kathi gave up entirely when Elizabeth turned 3 and emerged from our cabin doorway wearing a coonskin hat and an overly large camouflage shirt she had found in a closet. She dragged a toy wooden rifle. Then she looked at her stunned mother and demanded, "Where are the birds?"

I thought about this as the dogs romped through a large field the other day with Kevin and Elizabeth, while the older boys, Jon and Mike, searched with me for field mice in the corn.

Kevin sauntered over with his game pouch bulging. A chukar partridge was in there, even though there had been no shot.

"It was crippled, and Java found it and picked it up," Kevin explained.

But something truly important had happened. He had handed the still-living bird to his daughter, who now is 6.

"Ick!" she said, backing away. But Kevin gently thrust it into her hands and she felt the warmth of life. She looked anew at the splendid feathering.

"Cool," she declared, crossing another boundary.

Java wasn't around to strut her stuff when Jenna went to John Seyman's club last week for another hunting lesson. The puppy proved she has a way to go. She tracked down a couple of weak-flying released quail and proceeded to defeather them. Then she danced away with a bird in her mouth, refusing to deliver it.

"She's just playing," Seyman observed. "She needs some daily backyard work on basic discipline, just heeling and sitting and coming when she's called. If Kevin is too busy to do that every day, then Kathi should do it. The dog will learn faster and in a proper sequence."

I sit here, trying not to gloat. Dear Kathi. She really thought she had a grip on that anti-hunting thing. Now she'll be training a bird dog so her family can shoot wild game.

I know what's next, and so does she. I'll buy her a proper shotgun as soon as she is ready.

June 7, 1987

Beauty of nature in own backyard

Two weeks packed with unforgettable memories. . . .

Of the high country desert of northern New Mexico. Of snow-capped mountains with trout streams racing through fields of cactus and yucca.

Of golden eagles circling the breathtaking valley sweeps of the Rockies' western slope. Of grand vistas that stretch a hundred miles.

Of long, stony trails to pueblo ruins, still wearing petroglyphs drawn before Columbus unfurled his first chart of then-known seas.

Of hearing a geologist explain the colored bands of volcanic rock that dramatize the millennia involved in sculpting a canyon.

Experiencing the wonder of a desert thunderstorm. Of black clouds overpowering the horizon, bearing hail the size of golf balls, turning dry arroyos into surging rivers. Then subsiding in a flood of golden sunlight, the fresh wind sweet with sage and pinon, desert wildflowers popping amid the Remingtonesque colors of the west.

Good stuff. A fine vacation. With the promise of much more on future treks, now that you know the way to this wildness.

But were I to pick the best of the two weeks, there'd be no contest.

Home in the homely suburbs of Chicago. The tent pitched beneath a great oak in the back yard. The yard lights out, with only a flashlight to illuminate the mysteries of the night.

To a 3-year-old tenderfoot, this was extreme adventure.

Beyond the zippered flaps, we heard a kingdom of marauding raccoons.

True, they were feeding, as usual, at the neighbor's trough. But they paid courtesy calls at our tent. The boy heard padding and snuffling outside, and one came close enough to throw its shadow. These were wild, furry animals, and it was night and we were in their world.

But when Grandpa said it was OK, there was nothing to worry about. When the boy began to think of raccoons as fellow citizens of the world just trying to feed their families, he relaxed and listened and enjoyed.

The age of 3 is a good time for kids to start their journeys through the outdoors.

We'd actually begun a year ago, when the boy still was a toddler. We stumbled down a root-snarled path to a forest preserve creek and threw rocks and watched them make the water splash.

We learned to float sticks in the current, and to soak our feet and pants. One day, we turned over some rocks and invaded the world of bugs and allowed some to crawl on our hands. We suddenly were aware of the many life forms around us.

Through winter's snows, we'd search for tracks, and try to tell who made them. We'd snicker at the embarrassing idea of deer "pooping" in the woods, without wearing even diapers.

This spring we made a serious breakthrough. All by ourselves, without anyone prompting us, we peered into the creek mud and knew what we were seeing.

"Grandpa, a deer made that!" the boy announced. "And this. . . . a raccoon!"

It was time to do some camping.

We didn't want to venture far from the major conveniences, like Grandma, who'd be staying home to protect the baby brother. The distance of a holler to her bedroom window would be far enough. But we were becoming men now, and it was time to be more or less on our own.

The tent was crammed with pads and blankets and sleeping bags, for the night was blessedly cool. No bugs spoiled the party. No smothering humidity would keep us awake. We wore wool caps to keep our heads snug, and the flashlight glowed through the covers at our side. Only the raccoons were outside, and a dozen songs kept them and the shadows at bay.

Grandma, bless her, was ready at dawn. We crossed the street into the woods and found the path to her "secret log."

We cleared a spot on the ground for a fire and found the right size of twigs and branches. When the wood was reduced to coals, we put a grate atop a couple of rocks and heated an old iron skillet. The woods soon were full of the aroma of frying bacon. We made some toast and brought some juice and ate like kings, even the baby brother. And then we found a tree full of blackening mulberries and we picked dessert.

It would have been perfect except for the silly dog. She's a fine dog except for one big weakness. She absolutely loses her mind over fox scent.

Sure enough, she found a pile of fresh fox droppings and rolled in them and had to be tied up downwind. Grandpa was so mad, she didn't even get any bacon.

The camping was so much fun, we'll probably do it again in a couple of weeks. We'll go to a friend's farm when the thick hedges of raspberries are ready and we'll pick as many as we can eat.

We'll try not to scratch our hands and arms much, but even if we do, we won't let it bother us.

A few little scratches won't keep us from fishing for bluegills in our farmer friend's lake.

And we'll want to smell the corn growing in the fields, and the mud along the big river.

This is to be our summer of awakening.

CHAPTER SIX
AFTERNOON SHIFT

*John found adventure anywhere and everywhere, but he
was an especially ferocious advocate of Illinois and the
Midwest. He told anglers who dreamed of trips to faraway
places about the fabulous smallmouth bass fishing to be
found within a couple hours of Chicago, or the terrific
salmon fishing on Lake Michigan. When a new book told of
bird hunting across America, John grumbled that the author
had bypassed Illinois. "He needs to do a sequel," he said.*

*But John understood that wise management was key to
saving those places, not just for hunters and fishers but also
for hikers, bicyclists, canoeists and kayakers. When he saw
one of his state's precious natural sites slipping away, he
roared like a wakened grizzly, using the bully pulpit of his
column to sound the alarm. Among other achievements, he
is widely credited with pushing to turn the Joliet Arsenal into
the Midewin Tallgrass Prairie, and to turn the I&M Canal
into a protected greenway.*

*If you want to see John's monument, trek around his home
state. His legacy lives on in sites across Illinois and the
Midwest, protected for us all because John cared.*

April 5, 1987

7 years after starting in a valley, they finally have a mountaintop in sight

When the phone rang the other day and Jerry Adelmann's voice was chirping on the other end, I hoped it might be special news, and it was.

"It's all happening, John, just as we thought it could," he gloated. "The trails, the linkage. I can't believe it. It's finally coming together in our valley."

And as he talked, the years rolled back.

We first were tossed together in 1980, a young environmental activist with grand ideas and a somewhat battered sportswriter with a yen for the outdoors.

Jerry had been hired by Chicago's Open Lands Project to evaluate some wild lands and historic buildings along the Illinois-Michigan Canal in the Lockport area and he had found a treasure. He perceived the entire Des Plaines River Valley between Chicago and Joliet as a "hidden wilderness" of plant and wildlife habitat and recreational trails just waiting to be tapped by the 7 million residents of this metropolitan area.

He audaciously envisioned a new kind of linear park smack through an industrial corridor filled with railroads, canals, quarries, steel mills, tank farms, settling ponds, factories, power plants, barge lines and oil refineries.

Short of bombing, everything that could have been done to beat up the land had been tried in that valley. Yet, not even Chicago could completely use a valley so long and wide. For a hundred years, these managers and industrialists had done their best for commerce. Still, enormous pockets of wild prairies and forests and idyllic settings remained among the smokestacks and warehouses. Deer and furbearers abounded. The water trails had remained a flyway supporting 104 species of birds. With their fences and holdings, the factories themselves had protected much of the land.

Even more, these industries represented major contributions to society. Many were, in themselves, historic sites with unique technological properties, including some of the best remaining industrial architecture of their eras.

For 4 months, Jerry Adelmann and I prowled this valley. We brainstormed with hundreds of people from wildlifers and architects to bureaucrats and CEOs, and each person contributed another facet to the main idea.

The politicians got aboard quickly. Some saw this valley as a bold and valuable community service, potentially as brilliant in this day as the Burnham plan for the Chicago lakefront was in the last century. Only a city with the might and vision to set aside its lakefront for parks, to preserve thousands of square miles of invaluable forests and meadows, could conceive and deliver a beautiful park for millions through a valley of smokestacks.

The list of supporters was formidable. Sen. Charles Percy lined up the Illinois congressional delegation as well as Interior Secretary James Watt and rammed a bill through Congress forming a National Heritage Corridor administered by the National Park Service. Gov. James Thompson, Senate President Philip Rock and others did the honors in Springfield. The mayors and councils of dozens of towns along the waterways unified their support. The forest preserve districts of Cook, Will and Du Page Counties jumped aboard.

Regional, state and federal conservation, planning and waterway agencies provided major help. Most importantly, the Chicago Metropolitan Sanitary District—the largest landowner in the valley—assumed a leadership role.

I'll never forget the look from Nick Melas, the MSD president, when Adelmann and I sat down with his staff. We were a couple of wild-eyed zealots outlining a thing of dreams to people whose job was moving sewage. Some of them clearly thought us crazy. But Melas leaned back and squinted and we knew that he, too, had seen the vision. From then on, the project began to move.

Melas and his staff crafted a land-use approach to maintain the valley's vital role in area jobs and commerce, yet open ways for the public to behold the wonders hidden within. He saw a new way of promoting—even celebrating—sanitary districts, of showing off the world-renowned engineering feats that began in that valley decades ago by stringing trails through natural and historic sites. He saw that the wonderful Lockport Prairie was leased to the Will County Forest Preserve District.

Last Wednesday, the MSD's Centennial Committee, chaired by commissioner Gloria Majewski, saw for the first time a proposed link of hiking and biking trails between the Chicago Portage on Harlem Avenue and Lockport. They also reviewed proposals for a spectacular $55 million park and visitors center at the only point in the nation where three canals converge: the confluence of the I&M, the Sanitary and Ship, and Sag Channel between Willow Springs and Lemont.

Other systems are being crafted to tie Lockport to Joliet and the state's trail along the I&M Canal as far as La Salle. And other plans are being formed to link the I&M to the Illinois River and the Hennepin Canal, forming an unprecedented "Illinois Trail" that will cross the state.

If all goes well, by 1989 the MSD will celebrate its centennial by opening an unprecedented 23-mile recreational pathway that turns an industrial eyesore into a jewel. Chicagoans then will have much more than a lakefront and a series of forest preserve trails. They will have an historic pathway through their industrial might.

Eventually, these trails will reach all the way to Navy Pier and Calumet Harbor. The canals will offer water taxis. The ICG commuter railroad will add a new stop. Dozens of quarries–not to mention the ever-improving Chicago River–will be stocked with fish.

For perhaps the first time in history, an outdoor paradise will be provided by heavy industry. Seven years ago, how many of the environmentalists among us would dare to believe something like that?

Only one. Maybe two. And Jerry Adelmann, now executive director of the Upper Illinois Valley Association, still commits all his energies–as well as all he can wrest from a host of public and private agencies–to achieving it. Adelmann, through his group, remains the shepherd.

Bravo, Jerry. Call anytime.

May 5, 1993

Bountiful Root luring anglers

RACINE, Wis.—The Root River runs swift, heavy and brown in the spring, rushing the topsoil of southern Wisconsin farmlands into Lake Michigan.

For six miles from the impasse of Horlick Dam to its mouth near Racine, it carves through ancient limestone bedrock, grinding out a smooth, rocky bottom.

Here and there, gravelly riffles carve the water. And behind them lie snug holes packed with steelhead and salmon in season.

These fish were planted there, some 360,000 at varying times in the year, to circulate and grow in Lake Michigan. And each year, fulfilling the call of nature, surviving adults of six strains of trout and salmon return to spawn, creating, by far, the best wadable river fishery in the four-state southern basin of Lake Michigan.

Depending upon the nature of salmon and trout, these fish either die or move out to return in another year. In the meantime, they flood the river with steady runs of large and eminently catchable fish.

Right now, the Root is full of big steelhead, hard fighters as long as your arm. They weigh from 6 to 15 pounds and sometimes 20. They are so tough that anglers count battles almost as proudly as finished catches. On good days, the best can hook into 50 or more and catch maybe 20 or 25. For most mortals, however, three or four of these giants will do nicely, thank you. But there still will be 10 or 20 hookups.

The spring run consists of Chambers Creek and Ganaraska strain steelhead, one a native of Washington, the other from a tributary of

Lake Ontario. They stay through mid-May, when the river begins its only lull. By late June or early July, the summer-running Skamania steelhead arrive, peaking in the cooler waters of September and October.

There are fall runs of mature coho and chinook salmon ending their cycles, plus brown trout that drop eggs and return to the harbor. Then the Chambers Creeks and Ganaraskas come back, staying the winter. The Root also has heavy runs of sucker and carp, scads of stocked brook trout, fair populations of northern pike, crappie and largemouth bass, and even some walleye.

Matt Coffaro, a state fisheries technician, said the Root is special because all these fish concentrate within six miles of the dam. "We stock other rivers just as well, but their fish can be spread over many more miles," he said. "Those other steelhead rivers just don't have the action of the Root."

These steelies now bite fiercely into hooks tipped with fish eggs or colorful yarn flies that resemble eggs. They leap in startled flashes-thick cranberry rainbow stripes ablaze-as anglers wade gingerly through the treacherous current in pursuit.

Long, thin fly rods or other tough, light, flexible shafts bend and strain. Lines are heavier than you'd think you'd use for normal trout, tested for 10 and 14 pounds. But these, of course, are anything but normal trout.

"It's a world-class fishery, any way you look at it," said Don Dubin, a Root River expert from the Chicago suburb of Lincolnwood. He has fished the Root almost weekly for more than 20 years, watching it recover from a dank, polluted stream to become a classy, park-lined river that draws trout-mad fly casters from even the hotbeds of Montana.

"Except for that short lull for maybe six weeks from late May through June, this river is full of trout or salmon, and people can get to them," Dubin said. "It's a great fishery, a truly unbelievable fishery, and it's right here, an hour from home."

The Root now is swift and heavy from an unusually wet spring, but finally wadable. Anglers were stymied for three weeks last month by high water at what should have been the peak of fishing.

John loved to explore the woods.
Here he hunts in southern Illinois in 1997.

Often John joked that he wasn't much
of a fisherman, but some days it would
all come together.

John visited San Francisco often, and he loved to visit Fisherman's Wharf, where he sampled the local seafood.

Always a teacher at heart, John talked with Christopher Norville about land management and conservation in 1992 at the Turkey Trot Rod & Gun Club.

A caribou taken with a bow and arrow in Quebec in 1994.

John caught piranha on a trip to Venezuela—he enjoyed eating it.

1988, Inchon, South Korea . . . "the pure excitement of a thrilled and pounding heart."

John took some of his greatest joy in his family. His granddaughter, Elizabeth Coyle, got a helping hand while wading in Franklin Creek State Park, Illinois.

Picking apples was part of savoring nature's great smorgasbord.

Louise Husar, John's wife, became his partner in the field as well.

John didn't have to climb a tree to tower over most people, but he couldn't resist when playing with his grandsons Michael and Jonathon Coyle.

Of all John's many companions in the field, one of the best was Java, his black Labrador.

The Chambers Creek steelhead began to drop their eggs during that unfishable period. Now they mostly have spawned and are falling back toward the lake, resuming a normal feed. But the equally peppy Ganaraskas are at full spawn. At least another two weeks will pass before their primal urges decline and they, too, depart.

In the meantime—and especially on crowded weekends—anglers line productive reaches of the Root virtually shoulder to shoulder. Sometimes they have to cast in concentrated rhythms to avoid tangling lines.

Dubin and his buddies thought we needed to be on the water by 5 a.m. last Saturday to be assured of decent spots, and they were right. We were late, closer to 5:40, and three men occupied the prime riffle we had wanted, while four others were rooted farther upstream. But even settling for second spots, we almost immediately hooked into big fish. An hour later I glanced up to count 25 anglers wading a tight line within our two-block area.

Our spot was perfect for three hours, until the river suddenly dropped four inches. The force of the water perceptively lessened. At once, the fishing slowed.

"This is a current-driven fishery," Dubin explained. "The secret is knowing where to find the fish. When the water's up, they pile toward the dam and line the runs below. But when the water drops, they move back into somewhat deeper holes. Then we work farther down, closer to the mouth. Just now, the water has changed. The fish still are here. In fact, loads of fish are here, but they're much less active."

You couldn't tell that by watching Carl Rosenstein, Dubin's sidekick from Morton Grove. Eschewing a classical fly rod and reel for a whippy, 9-foot crappie rod and a modest Zebco 444 spincasting reel, Rosenstein stole the show, hooking 11 steelies, a brook trout, a pair of suckers and one fine carp, all on flies.

"And this wasn't even a very good day," he confessed.

Rosenstein ruefully had seen the anglers form their line smack amid a strong current one-third into the river. That, he felt, was where the fish wanted to be.

"I'm catching them in front of you," he announced, trying to be helpful.

He was letting the current drift his fly almost through his neighbors' boots, catching fish under their noses. A couple of times Rosenstein's fish swam right to me and seemed to pause, looking for help. He even took fish behind us.

"That's the problem with people being too close. Everybody gets in the way," he grumbled.

But everybody caught fish. One mustachioed fellow slowly prowled the opposite side, keeping out of casting range. He took three fish from shoreline runs that no one was working. Although many anglers use conventional rods and reels, spawn flies are the lures that work best for steelhead.

"This is an unreal fishery," Dubin proclaimed. "There's no place like it, and I've fished all over the world."

Especially unusual is the almost unlimited public access. Racine has built a network of city parks along the Root, with copious parking lots near prime runs. There is no reason why anyone cannot find a good spot to fish throughout the lower Root.

Just don't trespass on a golf club that fights litter with ticket-happy security guards. Stay in the water. After all, that's where the action is. Sometimes very unusual action.

For example, one guy felt a thumping on his boot. A steelhead was trying to spawn there.

June 14, 1992

Multifaceted Mackinaw inspires awe

CARLOCK, Ill.—The green hills of Woodford County rise tantalizingly toward puffs of tree-lined bluffs to the north.

The country roads wind up and down, torturously around and about, until they dive into the prettiest valley in all of central Illinois.

Be careful when you cross the Mackinaw River. Cars ahead invariably slow as drivers gawk. Wherever roads kiss this gorgeous prairie stream, the Mackinaw presents an irresistible face.

Riffles, sand bars, leafy overhangs, huge meandering bends. Each crossing reveals a different allure.

Solitary herons croak from translucent pools. Kids pole battered jon boats. Immense boulders are strewn across gravelly points where 50-foot glacial bluffs crumble before the hammer of time. Here the river rushes; there it seems to trickle. Now it is a lazy, southern backwater. Next you sense an alpine torrent.

The Mackinaw is revealed fully by canoe, from its narrow rise in McLean County through sublime enrichments from Money, Panther and Walnut creeks—all exquisite, if furtively hidden, natural waterways.

The river glides along, even in this time of drought. It moves in a steady fall. Ending in the Illinois River's bottoms near Pekin, it carves through gravelly Ice Age residues from its birth in the black soil beyond Bloomington. Its frequent drops make great rides for light craft. Canoes move just fast enough to challenge paddlers to find chutes without much danger when they inevitably do run aground.

We were well armed against danger last week. Mike Conlin, the state fisheries chief who cut his biological teeth on the Mackinaw, was showing off some of the river's treasures. We were fortified in an old steel canoe, the kind of solid, stable, barge-like craft that biologists use to keep from flipping when they scoop up samples.

This canoe had a mind of its own, and it seemed to know the "Mac" fairly well. Shove off and this armor-plated tank takes over. Steering becomes a form of negotiation. Should the canoe elect to go in an undesirable direction, you just paddle like maniacs and shout apprehensions. It turns as ponderously as a World War II sub passing through the mined nets of Tokyo Bay. We did just 13 miles in two days, and I've never paddled so hard and so fruitlessly. My arms and back will ache for days.

But it was an awesome introduction to a river I had wanted to float for years, but never seemed to have the time. Conlin has a fine way to explore the Mackinaw. He takes it in short, languid bursts between holes full of smallmouth bass.

We didn't paddle half a mile before we were beached upon a gravel bar, flailing jig spinners into the swift current. "What beautiful water!" Mike kept exclaiming, and there was no way even an irascible cynic could disagree. The Mackinaw winds almost continuously beneath tall, tree-shrouded bluffs, hidden from the prying eyes of man.

From gnarled benches and points, huge cottonwoods and sycamores screen a sense of dark forests rising up and out, presumably to the bean fields of harsh reality. Deep within its magical concourse, the Mackinaw provides serenity and solitude.

Not to mention an incalculable variety of plants and animals. While Conlin carried out the business of introducing himself to smallmouth after smallmouth, along with an array of snapping gar, white and rock bass and the richly hued longear sunfish, I chose to sit around, engulfed by bird calls.

The streamsides were full of plover, kingfishers, goldfinch, wood ducks, blue and green herons. At one point, we passed a dead cottonwood that held nine majestic turkey vultures, most still juveniles.

"I don't believe I've ever seen nine vultures in a single tree," Conlin sighed.

A beaver slapped the water beside our boat. Muskrats dove through woody tangles. In one productive hole, four large smallies broke the water beneath our noses.

Gar, bass, minnows, frogs and fry of all kinds churned the water before us. Various hens played the old broken wing trick to decoy us from their strings of ducklings.

We stopped five times in five miles, mostly to fish. By the second day, I let Mike do most of the fishing while I sat around and soaked in the sights and sounds of nature's perfection, just a little farther than two hours from Chicago.

At one stop, near the only barn along our route, I simply sat on a log and turned over rocks. I suppose I marveled at 35 insect species, while Mike admired the fish. In the busy world of today, who has the luxury of time to spend just turning over rocks?

We camped beside a rapids on a place belonging to a fellow who has let Mike study the river there for 25 years. By 1 a.m., we had burrowed through the woodpile, watching sparks flicker toward the Milky Way.

"After you get in tune with this place, you go home and hear the river for days," Mike said. "You hear it in your mind, as loud as it is now."

He took a sip of coffee and smiled. "Of course, I hear this river all the time. It only grows a little quieter after I've been away from it a while."

The state hopes to use part of the Mackinaw in its Pilot Streams Access Project, along with the Salt Fork of the Sangamon River. In a year or so, canoeable stretches will be designated, along with places to park and launch. Camping will be available at adjacent state parks.

"And there were people who wanted to drown this," Conlin said of a scuttled plan to dam the Mackinaw for a flood control reservoir. "Well, it's too beautiful a place to kill like that. This is one of the finest, most scenic and alive rivers in all of Illinois."

He demonstrated that with a pair of catches I found hard to believe. One was a toothy, 10-inch example of skipjack herring that has worked up the Mississippi and Illinois. Now it has found the Mackinaw.

Another was a 1-inch steel colored shiner, hooked in a bizarre little drama. Conlin had cast his Rooster Tail across a swift chute, when a smallie jumped at the bait. Then he reeled in the minnow, wriggling fiercely on the hook. The bass had taken a shot at the minnow, but the I told Mike I never had seen a minnow caught on hook-and-line and objected when he tossed it back into the stream.

It would have made a great mount, with an impressive ceremony in Springfield when the DOC lined up to present it to him for his wall. Just what every fisheries chief needs as a memento of his favorite stream.

JOHN HUSAR

December 3, 1986

Hunters are original protectors of wildlife

I got my fanny full of lead the other day for appearing to celebrate the killing of an elk.

I had written about the phenomenon of an escaped elk managing to survive a while in our state until some hunter finally mistook it for a deer.

Another writer leaped at the chance to demonstrate this as an example of the brutality of hunting. The implication, of course, was that hunting should be abolished or, if not, that hunters should have a crack at being the hunted.

My phones always go crazy when this happens, when a usually well-informed and always well-meaning colleague simplistically attacks the sport of hunting.

I hate it because I then have to honor the matter with a response. I don't like to tangle with people I like and respect, because I do understand the source of anti-hunting sentiment. Many, many good folks just can't stomach the idea of killing wild animals. I know. I used to be one.

But like so many lovers of wildlife, I hadn't understood how those creatures happened to be there in such proliferation.

I'd assumed that there always were deer in these woods, that geese circled local ponds every day. That rabbits and foxes and hawks lived in perennial balanced cycles. That the ducks always flew south, no matter what.

I'd forgotten about man.

Man is committed to progress, and progress always means expansion. That means new housing, larger cities, new industries, intensive farming, cutting forests, ditching streams, draining wetlands, tilling marginal soil, polluting the environment. In other words, wrecking the places where animals live.

Man is also by his nature a hunter, a seeker of food, and many rural people—even today—rely upon wildlife for their table.

Man is such a hunter that he killed off virtually all the whitetail deer east of the Mississippi by 1900.

He is so adept at the tools of progress that he wiped out billions of passenger pigeons simply by cutting away the contiguous forests they required for their unique form of survival.

But that was before we decided to put on the brakes.

The hunters themselves did it. Faced with declining game populations throughout the nation, they forced state and federal governments to assume responsibility for protecting and managing wildlife.

They did it because they wanted to save hunting.

To do it, they had to agree to do more than just put up virtually all of the dollars. They had to agree to be bound by stringent regulations covering hunting hours and seasons, bag and size limits, to mention just a few.

They agreed to cut off hunting for years, in some cases, while the wildlife populations were being rebuilt.

This massive effort involved the creation of various fish and wildlife agencies as well as departments of natural resources and conservation. To finance this, the hunters—and likewise the fishermen—agreed to be taxed for licenses that now include a variety of state and federal stamps for any number of conservation purposes.

They also agreed that excise taxes should be added to the cost of their firearms, shells and other equipment so that more monies could be poured into the management coffers. They formed thousands of chapters and organizations to raise funds to purchase or otherwise provide land for fish and wildlife. They stocked deer, protected geese, saved wetlands and caused governments to set aside millions of acres for nurseries and refuges. They introduced wild creatures like turkeys, otters, wolves and moose into areas that hadn't known their grace for generations.

They forced wildlife managers to do far more than hop around with baskets of furry creatures and fish eggs. They demanded solutions to the quandary of how to balance healthy wildlife environments with man's unquenchable thirst for progress.

All they asked was a chance to hunt when conditions were right.

So now we have huge herds of deer in every state. The Giant Canada goose no longer borders on extinction. Deer and geese, in fact, are coming out of our ears. They graze on our parks and lawns. They feast on crops like locusts and are nuisances in certain spots. Beavers clog our streams and rivers.

We have been hunting or trapping them legally for some time, under carefully regulated conditions. And still their populations soar.

Enlightened wildlife management—not to mention the money and restraint of hunters—continues to produce major wildlife gains despite man's continual assault upon the general habitat.

Hunters participate in that management by harvesting the abundance of game. By carefully shaping the hunting seasons, game managers allow—even encourage—hunters to take just enough of a harvest to ensure that reproduction overcomes natural mortality as well, and that the game populations will be stable.

Yes, we kill deer and rabbits and pheasants and geese and ducks. Yes, we hunt grouse and woodcock and prairie chickens and bear. And, yes, we enjoy the primal nature of the hunts as well as the wonderful food that we carry home.

We even like this food better than the food that is available in stores. We think that animals that spend noble lives foraging as part of nature make more relishing food than the untold unfortunates that never leave the feedlots or cages, that never taste a breath of freedom, that live only for slaughter and consignment to the grocery shelves.

At least in the hunter's quest, wildlife do win most of the encounters.

I could go on and on about nature and sport, of traditions and the human values in woodland skills, of the billions of dollars that hunting brings to our economies. I could quote philosophers on the nobility of the hunt.

But basically I am left to wonder why these anti-hunters are so against me selecting my own venison, or fooling a feeding or nesting fish, while it's okay to drive millions of commercial animals through the abattoir of a packing house.

I take enormous pleasure from hunting, even when I don't catch a thing. Hunting lures me outdoors into a primal contest with nature, and the things I see and do mark me as a man.

I know of no hunters who do not love wildlife enough to spend big money and enormous hours every year to make sure that it is there.

Until the anti-hunters take over and pay the freight and begin to do the grunt work, hunters chiefly will continue to be responsible for providing wildlife.

Anti-hunters should keep that in mind when they strive to eliminate hunting. Succeed and, in time, they will eliminate the very wildlife that they profess to love.

All of those fees and taxes that carry wildlife management will dry up. Organizations like Ducks Unlimited, Pheasants Forever, Quail Unlimited and the National Wildlife Federation no longer will raise millions annually to improve habitat.

With no legal hunters, there will be no need for wardens to enforce game laws. Stocking programs will end and protection will cease. In time, the poachers will kill everything that's left. They'll turn again to the eagles, hawks and many songbirds. The frogs and turtles will be eaten. We'll have lost everything that we've gained.

And Bambi will remain exactly what he is—a humanized character in the storybooks.

October 20, 1994

Experience our wetlands—naturally

Preach all you wish about precious wetlands. But you'll never know the spirit of those babies until you slog toward a duck blind in the blackness before dawn, hoping you won't be lost or drowned.

To many duck hunters—who take to the marshes in northern Illinois on Thursday—wetlands are flooded grain fields that have been pumped full of water. That's what we are reduced to, with most real wetlands drained, farmed or developed away. The phony ones are easy to navigate—just stay on the berm or levee surrounding the field. Be careful you don't tumble into someone's camouflaged pit or blind.

But natural wetlands are creatures unto themselves. They are independent systems configured by higher intelligence. They smell of rich mud and teem with animal and plant life. You pick your way through real marsh grasses in thin, flat, tippy boats, brushing tree limbs aside. Eyes strain in the darkness for familiar landforms and trees. If wading is possible—or mandatory—you plow through shallow water pushing a jon boat piled with decoys, coffee and shotguns, and hope you won't step into a hole.

Wetlands can be great fun if the mud is thick. I once walked out of a pair of rubber chest waders while pushing a boat through Coon Creek. I later entertained some hunting buddies in a Mississippi rice field when I left a hip wader two steps behind me.

If you time things right, you'll reach your blind just as the horizon is streaked with dawn's first gray light. Then you wade around the chilly water, untangling decoys from their anchor cords. You toss them in carefully planned patterns based on the wind and the ducks' anticipated inward flight. If you lay the floating decoys right, ducks that spot them from the air will think there's a comfy opening right where a lot of other ducks are feeding. They'll swing over once or twice—if they're cautious, seven or eight times—then drop to the water within easy range of the guns, hopefully 20 to 35 yards.

Of course, you never get the decoys right at first. The growing light reveals some floating upside down, others tangled in anchor cords. Back you go, correcting things, sometimes just when the first flight of ducks wants to come in.

I loved to watch one pal, a perfectionist in these matters, crouch among the bulrushes while we highballed ducks around him like parachutes from the sky. We would shoot half our limits while he would hunker in full view as still as possible, cursing fate in a nasal monotone that fortunately sounded like an excited drake. With him out there, we didn't even need a dog. He would retrieve the ducks on his way back to the blind.

When things were slow, we would send him out to fool with the decoys, hoping his rotten luck would bring in more ducks.

Normally, everything is set before legal shooting begins, which is half an hour before sunrise. Woe to the hunter who breaks that embargo. Game wardens seem to lurk behind every cattail. If not today, they will tomorrow—because miffed sportsmen do report illegal early shooting.

Good duck hunters do not shoot before light is strong enough to identify sex and species. With a crisis in duck numbers because of marsh losses throughout the continent, hunters are limited to specific numbers and species in various flyways.

Mostly, you sit and wait and listen. You sip coffee and murmur softly among yourselves, transfixed by the golds and magentas of a dawning sky. Trees and grasses magically gain definition. Songbirds swirl. Beaver and muskrat police their areas before going to bed. As the day warms, a water snake may carve a path through green mats of duckweed along shore.

I once shared a duck blind with wildlife artist Richard Timm, and that was a day to remember. All duck hunters should see their marshes through an artist's eyes. Timm saw much more than soft light and flowing cattails. He photographed the grain of the wooden beams of the blind. He noticed the sunlight in a dog's eyes.

When I later bought one of his artist's proofs—a scene of geese darting above a broad, slate-misted backwater slough—I told him it had to have been painted on Snicarte Island in the Illinois River.

"No way" Timm said. "That's Minnesota's Mille Lacs."

I gave him a glare. And to this day I tell my friends this is how hunting looks along the lower Illinois. The truth of art remains in the eye and heart of this particular beholder.

JOHN HUSAR

May 1, 1991

A true confession of burning desire

To each his peccadillos. In the slightly surreal world of outdoors, people happily sit through drenching rains to hook a mess of fish that no one wants to clean.

Fun equals five or six motionless hours in a fly-swarmed tree stand on the outside chance that a bear will sniff the smelly bait below. Prudence is letting a Lyme-infected deer tick scuttle across your nose—knowing that any motion might scare away that keen-eyed turkey behind a bush.

Joy is breaking ice in a shallow duck pond so you can drag a boat full of decoys through the inky blackness of a muddy marsh and return without frostbite.

We all have our strange tastes.

I'll confess to another: Tramping through old farms in the spring, burning fields.

I call it my ritual of springtime rejuvenation. My wife calls it pyromania, but even she gets out there, raising smoke.

We claim to be naturalists, helping the land recover from the intrusion of man. In fact, we like to watch fires cleanse those fields and feel the power of instigating nature's processes.

We burn cornstalks and dried milo with their distinctive perfumes. We ease fire through dried meadows, burning away a year's debris. We thin the fields of sunlight-blocking weeds and leave a coat of nutritious mineral ash to feed the 'good' plants that will follow.

If things are timed right, spring rains quickly rejuvenate the stored seeds and deep roots of long-hidden native plants, and they win the race to the surface. The charcoal becomes carpeted by green shoots and blossoming wildflowers. Then come the slender, swaying grasses that the Indians and early settlers knew. These are prime home and food for the animals of the field, from mice and rabbits to quail, foxes and hawks.

Burning lets us play another version of the hunting game, the strategy of man versus nature. There is no room for mistakes when working with fire. You constantly read the winds. You carefully gauge border strips wide enough to keep the blaze from jumping. You work the fire slowly into the wind. When it's safe, you rake the fire forward in a narrow strip, then across its advancing line. You let it rage back upon itself, consuming blocks of grass, saving time, but always in control.

For us it is recreation. Louise and I have burned 24 acres in five fields this spring, some for the first time. Now we wait to see what comes up. Will there be surprise wildflowers? Will the switchgrass grow stronger, as predicted? What will flourish in those corn strips that are being taken out of production?

The members of Turkey Trot Rod & Gun Club, who run this old farm, have strong ideas about agriculture and nature. They don't permit chemicals, except a little nitrogen on the few strips of corn grown to pay taxes and feed deer. That means no pesticides or herbicides whatsoever. Our fields enjoy weeds and bugs-not to mention worms and butterflies, snakes and rabbits. Our well water is fit to drink.

We raise insects for baby quail to eat, and our fields are gardens for the moles and woodchucks. We want pheasants nesting in every field and trees and bushes that sag of berries, apples and walnuts. There should be more walnuts than our squirrels can eat.

A year ago, we burned some narrow woods along fencelines and cornerpoints. While a few Turkey Trotters were leery at first, they soon appreciated the chance to chase pheasant and quail through those woods without shredding skin and clothes. Controlled fires are 'cool' fires, you see, and do not harm large old trees. They clear away the thorny understory and replace brambles with beds of grass. Wildflowers abound where the sun hadn't smiled.

There are good and bad times for burning, of course. Early spring is best to clear brushy intrusion. Later fires kill the first shoots of fast-growing weeds, freeing space for more desirable plants. While some burning can harm wildlife nests, the improved habitat outweighs those risks. Animal populations benefit immensely over time.

In one strip the other day, a dozen field mice hopped through the charred debris in search of their burrows. Without cover, many soon would become dinner for owls and coyotes. But most strips were left untouched. Every strip in every field should not be burned each year.

Fire management follows the principles of hunting and fishing. Improve the living conditions of animals and they flourish. Remove an excess deer or two and a few meals of rabbits, squirrels and game-birds and you're making room for forthcoming babies. The trick is to leave plenty of stock for the population to recover. At Turkey Trot, that's hardly a problem. Conservationists agree today that top priority must go to habitat enhancement, especially in Illinois. Modern farm-ing and urban development have weakened many natural processes here.

Big industrial farms hold few diverse pockets of nature. Wetlands are drained to squeeze a few more bushels of corn. Trees are cut in marginal areas. Homes and businesses are built in flood-prone river bottoms, then the hapless rivers are reduced to ditches. Vacation homeowners convert lakeside habitat to sterile lawn, then wonder where the ducks and other birds went.

At Turkey Trot the other evening, Louise and I saw 10 deer nosing for charred grains of corn. Pheasants cackled everywhere. Blossoms were sweet and full on the trees. We had a beer on the porch as the night sounds engulfed us. Make burning a sport and we'd have felt like champions.

CHAPTER SEVEN
SUNSET

John once grumped to a friend about the expectations people had for outdoor writers. He had been in a small Illinois town the night before the pheasant season opened, and a bunch of hunters had gathered at the local trap range for some last-minute practice.

"I got up there to shoot and everybody got quiet," John moaned. "They wanted to see the expert in action."

John would have been the first to tell you he was no expert. He got his fishing lures tangled in tree branches just like everyone else. Thick eyeglasses made it hard for him to see a speeding clay target, much less hit it. And if you talk to John's hunting and fishing pals, before too long they will tell you a hilarious story about the big guy falling into the river, or breaking through some ice.

Yet when it came to appreciating the world and its wonders, John really was an expert. John saw extraordinary things no matter where he found himself, and as the world roared around him, he squeezed out quiet moments when he could stop and smell the roses.

December 6, 1995

Honor and pride uncompromised by lousy hunt

This was not my best deer hunt. I had seen more than a dozen white-tails, but most were moving or out of sporting shotgun range. I won't shoot at moving deer. It's unethical to try a chancy shot.

One silent eight-pointer had stopped 15 yards to my side while I hunkered like a frozen lump on a plastic bucket with my gun propped against a tree. I had been munching an apple. The deer fixed his eyes on me for a minute while I tried not to breathe. Then he wheezed once, danced to the side and plunged safely across a creek.

An even bigger rack jumped a neighbor's fence at sunset during the first season and I took a whack from 40 yards with my wife's gun, my own being out of commission. I missed badly and vowed to have my gun fixed by last weekend.

A nice doe edged within 30 yards of my scent field—the first doe I had ever summoned with a male grunt call. When she didn't find her buck, she began edging away. It was now or never. I forced a shot through some twigs and the slug was badly deflected. She loped away without a scratch.

Last Saturday, a herd of deer stole past my ground stand in the predawn gloom. It was too dark to try a shot. They sniffed and pawed and jumped the fence and were gone. That was the story of my season.

But a little more than an hour later, five deer stopped at a rocky ford near my spot. I was wedged between a dead tree and a fallen log with a beautiful view of a creek and forest.

Two grown fawns crossed the creek, followed by a large doe. Two more followed. This being the sixth of seven days of firearm hunting allowed in Illinois, I now was hunting for the table. The big doe would be prime venison and her fawns were old enough to fend for themselves. Good hunters carefully pick and choose their shots. I have been proud most of my kills never took more than seven or eight steps. But now and then you just make a lousy shot. Then you are obligated to follow a wounded and possibly dying deer.

I watched with sickening dismay as the five deer, trailed by my wounded doe, ran hard along the creek bank and out of sight.

The last time I had to follow a blood trail, the young buck was dead within 75 yards. That's reasonably acceptable. Dying, for any creature, rarely is as clinical as old shoot-'em-up western films depict.

I gave her time to lie down and hopefully die nearby. Then I began the real hunt, the sleuthing after sometimes tiny droplets of blood on leaves and twigs and patches of remnant snow.

It took me half an hour to cover 100 yards and the deer still was moving well. I saw where she crossed the creek and entered a public park. Because you just don't carry shotguns in parks, I gave my gun to my son-in-law, Kevin Coyle, and continued the search. Half an hour later, I spooked the deer from a deep ravine and watched her top a ridge and head toward a county road. She would cross the road, I thought. All I could do was go back, get my gun, and drive around the park to the other side.

We wolfed a snack at the cabin and changed boots, giving the deer more time to settle down. Then Kevin and I drove the county road looking for blood along the shoulder where the deer had crossed. We found none. We walked the road and the edge of a farmer's field and saw nothing. The doe still had to be in the park.

Kevin and I struck off in different directions, hoping to find where the doe had left the ravine. I finally found a place that seemed familiar, spotted a major deer path, walked 30 yards and came to a splotch of fresh blood.

But in 15 minutes of pacing in ever-widening circles, Kevin and I could find no more. We chose a likely direction and trailed different paths. Ten minutes later, our hearts stopped as a doe bolted from some underbrush and lay down beside a log. And there we were with no gun.

"You stay with the deer and keep it from spooking back down that deep ravine," I told Kevin. "I'll get my gun."

I knew the law was somewhat ambiguous about this. You don't hunt in closed areas of parks. But the state also recognizes a moral obligation to pursue and humanely destroy a wounded animal. Because I had located the deer and feared it would be lost, I was certain I was doing the right thing.

I found Kevin's blaze orange hat and his urgent hand signals directed me toward the deer. It took two shots, but the hunt finally was done after three hours of painstaking search. I apologized to the deer's spirit and thanked her for feeding my family. Kevin then took my gun back to the truck while I tagged and cleaned the carcass. Then we tied it to a pole and hauled it about 400 torturous yards to the county road.

As I said, this hunt had not been my best. My shot had failed by four inches from being an instant kill. A noble deer needlessly suffered.

But Kevin and I at least could be proud we hadn't quit. We twice had lost the blood trail, but we persisted. We honored that deer, we satisfied the Code of the Hunt, and we thankfully did not dishonor ourselves.

November 5, 1995

Spare ducks,
and bag satisfaction

The magic of duck hunting begins in the dead of a drizzly night, when trucks and vans rumble into a crowded barnyard near a musty marsh. The dogs leap out, scouring through underbrush, sizing up each other, quickly forming packs.

The men stretch and rummage at their tailgates, donning waders, swilling home-brewed coffee, checking guns and shells. Someone tests a duck call, but quietly. The night must not be sullied by rushing dawn.

Inside the barn, in a bright, stuffy side room, hunters face each other from wooden benches against the walls. It reminds you of a prizefighter's dingy dressing room, of the tiny warrens set aside for visiting basketball teams. They munch doughnuts or coffeecakes and talk of ducks they have seen on other lakes.

The walls are predictable. Ribald cartoons of ducky doings tilt in ratty frames. Tired homilies, including rules and warnings, glare from marker-scrawled cardboard. Faces of long-gone duck hunters beam from yellowed photos, piles of ducks at their feet. We certainly don't kill ducks like that anymore.

At Jim Scheer's barn near Wilmington, a placard proclaims the fine for unethically killing a mallard hen at $20, scratched down from $50. "When it was $50, no one ever paid," Scheer grumps.

In a clanging, metallic voice, he ordains that hunters in his blind this year can shoot three mallards, and maybe a teal or pintail or other bonus duck that happens by. Nothing like the official five-duck bag limit authorized by the feds. A lifelong eccentric who has contributed—and wrung from friends—bushels of money for water-fowl causes, Scheer thinks he can protect ducks better than the feds.

He clearly is pleased when his son, Tim, announces that his blind will have a three-duck limit–and no bonuses. The hunters nod their obedience. It's best not to play the role of meathog around these Scheers, or you'll need to find another place to hunt your ducks.

It's getting light, nearly half an hour before sunrise. We should be in our blinds by now and ready for legal hunting hours. Instead, we're still in the barnyard, hefting selves and dogs into the backs of trucks. Scheer doesn't go to his ponds early. He doesn't like to push ducks off the water when it's dark. He wants them to stay on the farm, to find an accommodating pond nearby, and for this he thinks they need to see. Hunts thus start at Scheer's about half an hour late.

"It's easier to identify the ducks by then, anyway," he shrugs.

Besides, the joint always is loaded with ducks. We ride in procession on a gravel road, trucks peeling this way and that to reach scattered ponds. We rumble past flat, silent waters teeming with dark blobs of waterfowl, a camouflaged military convoy on maneuvers.

On the other side of the farm, where cornfields have been flooded, the truck stops along a fencerow. Four of us and a dog march toward our assigned pond. Atop a rise, our breathing stops. At least 300 ducks and geese sit on the water.

Slowly, the birds take notice. A few lift off the pond, followed by others. Soon the air is black with rising ducks and geese. And still others sleep in the back reaches of the pond. They finally leave when we wade out with the decoys. That's one of the anomalies of duck hunting. You chase away 300 birds so you can float some fake ones in hopes of luring them back.

Scheer never lets his guests shoot into large flocks. You educate too many ducks that way. He picks at singles, doubles and triples. No more than five or six. Be sure the head is green, the sign of males. Scheer has another rule. Kill a hen and you're through for the day.

He and his old pal, Ron Desederi, thought they were drawing beads on two males. Wham! Wham! Two ducks dropped into the cornfield behind the blind.

"I think you got a hen there, Ron, and I got the male" Scheer chortled.

The dog came back with two hens. Scheer unloaded his gun, honoring his own rule.

"Trouble is, I don't know who to pay the $20 to," Scheer grumbled, acknowledging his current ire at various waterfowling groups, his normal recipients of largesse. He thinks they compete too much instead of helping ducks.

For two hours, ducks fly consistently on these impeccable acres. Whenever they settle into the decoys, the shooting is easy.

Scheer worries that some ducks can detect faces in his blind. He wonders if we should put up the flipper, a straw screen on a low hinge that closes the pit.

The trouble is, unless you have X-ray eyes, you can't see the marsh with the flipper in your face. I want to see the marsh. Scheer and Desederi want to lure some ducks. Scheer's grandson, Robert Schmidt, is just happy to be there.

"If you can't see the marsh, the magic of hunting ducks is gone," I bleat. "With the flipper up, it's like sitting in a tomb."

After a while, Scheer counts the ducks and arbitrarily decides we've harvested enough. "Two birds each, plus a pintail," Scheer clangs. "That's it. Let's get the decoys."

We've seen hundreds of ducks, and bagged a few. We've had a marvelous hunt. We are happy conservationists. We spare the rest.

On our way out, the sodden day begins to warm. It is good to be in an Illinois marsh with fine sportsmen who deeply care, who revere the birds they hunt, who gladly practice restraint. The coffeecakes await.

June 8, 1994

"Alone" on island? Yes, but that doesn't mean lonely

CRANBERRY PORTAGE, Manitoba—I finally grabbed some time on a piney Canadian island.

Totally alone. Just me and a few thousand unacquainted creatures around a lichen-covered rock with 40 or 50 wind-whipped trees.

You know the place. One of those untouched, lonely, delicious islands we always hurtle past while racing to another fishing spot.

For years and years on trips to the North Woods, I've yearned to tie the boat to a picturesque island and just hunker down. To effectively stop the world and get off. To sit still and maybe sense the immensity of where I was.

I've always been too pressed to feed that yen. There were fish to find, camp schedules to meet, partners to consider. You don't find many fishing buddies willing to kill hours on a rock, just to indulge a fellow's mind.

But now I'd borrowed a boat after supper and snooped around until I found the perfect landing. Five tiny islands formed a little midlake harbor just three miles from the dock at Tonapah Lodge. A deep reef hooked them to islands across the way. Now, at last, sighing with exquisite satisfaction, I lay upon a rounded dome of bedrock and lose myself within the cobalt sky.

I am overwhelmed by the infinite variety of colors in the clouds. If Eskimos have 26 words to describe distinctly different snows, I face the same challenge for wisps of crystallized moisture above this far-away lake amid the golden hours before sunset.

Penetrating cries of loons chortle all around. Out here, loons run the show. They barely tolerate passing boats, eyeing intruders suspiciously, diving if one drifts too near. Loons are magnificent divers, able to stay below as long as 18 minutes, processing oxygen from air stored in hollow bones. When they believe they are alone, inhibitions roll away. A community of five paired loons now converses hotly, unaware of my prying ears.

My rock hosts six kinds of lichen. Stare hard and they become Lilliputian forests, colored confederate gray to duckbill orange to four hues of green.

The crassly commercial red and green of my boat ordinarily might seem foreign, save for the fact that the boat is old and battered like these timeworn slabs of rock-cracking, shifting, minutely eroding from each slap of waves.

The water is as alive as the rocks with plants and insects. A steady gaze from just the right angle reveals a skin of swarming microscopic plankton on the lake's otherwise crystal surface. Creatures inch past the island, propelled by the steady current of an ancient river system that chains lake to lake.

Now and then a large insect floats past, benignly riding the current, unaware of its place in the food chain. Our lives briefly intertwine. Then I hear a splash off the reef and know a fish has ended our acquaintanceship forever. And then a gull drops low to scoop up a piscine morsel. Thus life goes on.

I lie back again, immersed in the depths of space beyond the clouds. Last night the Northern Lights flamed above. I think how nice it would be to camp upon this rock the very night those Lights appear.

A raven calls from the peak of a pine, intelligent enough to mimic human sounds. If I lived here, we might tame each other.

A boat ambles by, its people pretending not to notice me. The ravens are friendlier.

I find a bathtub-sized recess in rocks against the shore. Too bad the evening has become chilly or I'd be naked and neck-deep in water.

It's jacket time. The sun pulsates in gleaming ripples off a rocky shelf that slides into the deep. The eastern sky erupts in salmon and raspberry.

A swift boat creates a mini-surf that washes my sneakers and scours and cleanses my island. Half a mile across the water, waves pound another shore, producing the illusive roar of distant rapids. The imagination soars.

Another boat breaks my reverie. Now I know how those loons must feel.

The airhorn of a train reverberates through the distance. That, too, is the stuff of dreams, the storied mixed train to Lynn Lake, cutting through muskeg and forest, snaking past wilderness lakes. Someday I'll just stop the world again and see where it goes.

Civilization has beckoned. An ash tumbles from my fine cigar, rolling intact down the rock, sizzling when it hits the water. Another human desecration.

A row of thunderheads rises in the distance, and one bears the formidable warning shape of an anvil. Even romantics must leave the water.

I hope I'll soon "waste" another evening on an island again.

JOHN HUSAR

July 20, 1994

Taking our sweet time can enrich body and soul

Time gallops faster and faster.

In the sweet bygones of boyhood, summers stretched endlessly from May to September. Now I never know what happened to the days. I'm invariably surprised to note the month I'm in. I rip off the pages of my calendars a week or two or, sometimes, three late. I miss things-good things like loosely scheduled fishing trips-because I lose track of time.

Here it is, the middle of July, and I'm still mentally fooling around with May's fishing patterns.

What happened to the spawn and the post-spawn? How do you blow off a month or two?

This is an age when time is a more precious commodity than money, when immense energies are jammed into the competitive process of making a living. Time is spent in huge amounts to stay ahead or just stay abreast. There is less for leisure, for squandering supine in prairie grasses just to hear the symphonic swish of wind.

Remember how we used to kill an hour prowling fields, watching clouds form, scanning skies to guess at the morrow's weather? As if the morrow's weather now matters. Most of us likely will be back at work, immersed in the grind of life. What suckers we have become.

That point was driven home the other day on a sweet farm I often haunt in western Illinois. In just three weeks of teeming growth, the back roads and woodland lanes became nearly impassable. We used to be able to drive anywhere without gouging paint from the sides of the truck. In three weeks, like clogging arteries, that world grew tighter, narrower. It's the story of modern life.

I went there on a Sunday to scout the deer paths and dove fields and to revel in summery swarms of wildflowers. I happened to come back three days later and found swarms, all right—the thickest clouds of mosquitoes since a long-ago summer in humid south Texas.

All those recent thunderstorms did their job. While the farmers seem happy, the rest of us must steer clear of lowland woods without at least a Canadian-style bug jacket.

Just three days made an immense difference.

That same farm, the same day, unveiled another compression of time.

Four weeks earlier, I'd had the thrill of my first encounter with a new flock of wild turkeys. My wife earlier had seen a hen or two in different fields, and this spring spotted some chicks being herded across an adjacent county road. Now it was my turn. The truck had turned onto a short lane between two fields when I slammed the brakes at the spectacle ahead.

Two turkey hens calmly walked along the lane, herding at least a dozen gray chicks. Three or four chicks bobbed in line behind their mothers. The others sprang up and down between ground and tree limbs, horsing about like playful adolescents, testing the miraculous new strength in their wings.

I watched them bob and flutter out of sight, then backed the truck onto another lane and took a longer route back to the farmhouse. Now, four weeks later, on a sandy lane behind the barn, swatting more and more mosquitoes with each disconsolate step, I was jarred by a sudden, thunderous burst of noise.

Three dark bodies erupted from a grassy hillside not 30 yards away. My dog leaped and fell back. I thought she was having a heart attack. What could they have been? Hawks? Owls? Vultures?

Then more eruptions came from the tree line above the hill. Two black bodies tore through the woodlot. Then three more from another tree. Then more.

I realized what they were before I saw the first flying silhouette. This farm had been enriched with a flock of now-immense wild turkeys. They'd been in the trees to sit out a summer storm. True, they were mostly juveniles at the moment, but give them a couple more months. Give 'em a year or two and turkeys will roost and scratch throughout these woods.

So time flies with several degrees of relevance. It took us three years from the initial county stocking to see turkeys on this farm. It took a month for babies to become semi-adults. It took a couple of sorely needed rainstorms to create a three-day hatch of mosquitoes that drove us inside.

It probably will take a serious lifestyle change to give us back a bit of the commodity of time that we spent so freely in youth. And we need that time desperately now to give our responsibility-crazed lives proper meaning and succor.

JOHN HUSAR

November 1, 1995

Mr. October says fond farewell to swiftest month

And yet another October is finished. How long did it last? Ten minutes? Two days? Maybe a week?

October really needs another 40 or 50 days. Just so we can fill ourselves with its succulence.

To outdoors folk, October is the sweetest and swiftest month, the apex of the year. April is also up there. But while April's greening promise heralds the months ahead, everything climaxes in October. And there's no way fools like me can have it all.

Then it's gone. The wheel turns and winter settles in. November has its glorious deer and pheasant moments, its Indian summer, but October deals with everything that can be done without parkas and snow boots.

Think about the summer. Hot and muggy. And maddeningly buggy. Full of people in the parks and on the lakes. Summer means messy campsites, boat trailers everywhere and crowded bike paths.

Finally comes the change of September. School starts and the crowds leave resort country. The cottages are boarded up. Still, the nights can be sweaty and bugs remain hungry. September is only a period of awaiting October's first frosty nip.

And, finally the trees begin their spectacular dramas. Bugs leave and the undergrowth dries away. The forests open to idle tramping. Hikers and cyclists click off mileage in cool comfort and happy solitude. Campsites open everywhere, and the perfume of maple and hickory fires graces the country air.

In October, hunting expands beyond those sweaty days of

September's early teal and doves, and squirreling that no one does because the leaves are too thick. Ducks and grouse come into season and deer archers await the beginnings of rut.

For anglers, October heralds the fall feeding frenzy, when fish binge upon the summer's leavings to build a supply of fat to carry them through winter.

On the big waters of Lake Michigan, huge salmon and trout school close to shore and spawners crowd the lakeside streams.

The biggest muskies grow ravenous in October, hungry river walleyes stream toward the dams, catfishing is hottest at mid-day, and the ponds and lakes produce their biggest panfish.

What would I do if I could have several months of Octobers?

I would spend one of those months strictly in Illinois, saluting the northern smallmouth streams, canoeing in leafy splendor. I'd spend a morn scouting deer in glimmering forests, then head for the Mississippi River and its walleye and sauger at the dams. I'd camp in primitive state sites near Yorkville and float the Fox River for fishing and scenery. I'd bike the Hennepin and I&M canals. I'd look for ducks and geese in the potholes of northern counties and, by the end of the month, ensconce myself in some secluded backwater of the Illinois River for the Central season duck opener.

With another October, I'd tramp through Upper Michigan and northern Wisconsin for muskie and grouse. I'd kiss away the end of the year in rustic byways and bucolic tank towns with small cafes and supper clubs and long memories of great guides and record fish and historic fishing waters. I'd watch the leaves turn from Minnesota on down and duck hunt my way home.

I'd spend a third October entirely within the Rockies, decoying antelope in Montana, elk hunting in Colorado, prowling the arid canyons of New Mexico. I'd take up a buddy's invitation to sit on his mountaintop in Idaho. I'd fly-fish every stream I saw for luscious mountain trout. I'd float the Snake and the Gunnison. I'd camp in the Grand Canyon and in the ultra-remote Deep Creeks of western Utah.

And now the jangling phone shatters this reverie. A young mother of three wants to know what in the world she can do with her kids. I fumble for practical thoughts. She doesn't want to hear me muse of grouse hunting in Wisconsin or fly floating the Gunnison.

The easy copout is to point her toward some place to fish. But that can be poor advice. Unless she knows how, fishing by inexperienced parents and kids can be misery. They may not find any fish. And if they do, she may not have rigged the lines in any way that fools the fish. Her only hope is finding a kindly bait shop operator who'll do the rigging for her.

What I'd tell her is to drive to any state park or wildlife area, get a map and walk around. Check the bulletin board for special activities. Ask the ranger for some tips.

Do this four or five times and she and the kids will discover some interests they never knew they had. They'll have questions that need on-site answers. They'll discover trails and overlooks and fishing docks that will draw them back.

And, of course, there's one more thing. I'd tell them to be sure to do this next October.

JOHN HUSAR

May 20, 2000

Getting lost in the wild makes for wild tales

A doctor was studying the scars on my chest and wanted to know what had happened to my nipple.

"Did you have surgery there?" she asked. "Did someone biopsy it?"

My face flushed. The blame, I said, belongs to an insensitive Missouri jumping mule. I was aboard one of those stalwart creatures on a raccoon hunt late one night when it plowed straight through some thorn bushes.

Thorns apparently are little more than itch relief for thickly hided mules. Or perhaps mulishly secret ways of brushing off unwanted 250-pound human payloads.

Anyway, once we bulled through, my shirt and chest were shredded. I was too dumb and mulish to let myself be flung down to where I might crawl beneath the thorns.

Well, you live and learn—if you live. At least I wasn't lost. I knew precisely how many miles I would have to hike and crawl in the dead of night to get back to the pickup trucks. Maybe that's why I stayed on.

You do whatever it takes to keep from being lost in the wild. I quail at the idea of winding up like those unfortunate buddies, one of whom got sentenced last week for the mercy killing of his injured friend while lost in the desert of Carlsbad Caverns National Park. I've been lost a few times—truly lost—on wilderness bear hunts in Canada and I've never wanted that trauma repeated.

One's chances aren't great. About 10 percent of hikers and hunters who get lost in the Canadian wilderness never are found, mainly because they keep on walking–often the wrong way—instead of hunkering in a clearing, building a smoky fire and waiting to be found.

I had to laugh last week when I reposed on the bank of a country creek in western Illinois and heard a father on a footpath urge the kids to stay close "or you'll get lost."

Fat chance of that in civilization. This narrow little state park is confined to the creek's meanders. Go too far either way and you're either on a farm or in someone's backyard. Any kid who knows how to ring doorbells would be back at the park office within an hour.

I will confess to being turned around a few times in places like Palos Woods and even Turkey Trot Rod & Gun Club. Palos encompasses 14,000 acres in southern Cook County, and if you do get mixed up, you still can walk a couple of miles until you hit a road.

Turkey Trot's maze of fields and woods are much easier for novices. Just walk until you reach a fence, then turn around and walk back. Eventually you'll find the barn.

The Canadian bush is another world. Go the wrong way on a moonless night or a cloudy day with hidden sun and, if you're really persistent and stupid and unlucky, you may reach the Arctic ice cap. Of course, by then you better have developed a caribou's taste for moss and lichen because that's about all you'll find in the way of food.

Unless it's cranberry and blueberry season, but that means it's also mosquito season and you'll be drained of blood and consumed by bears within a week. So don't worry about chow.

The first time I got lost up there was near Thaddeus Lake in Ontario. My partner, Spence Petros, thought he had arrowed a bear at twilight and it was after midnight by the time we found our outfitter and began our search. We should have known we were in trouble when the outfitter arrived with a yapping mutt and a .22 rifle, hardly enough firepower for raccoon, let alone wounded bear.

We wandered the bush in circles as the dog led us on big loops that brought us back to the tree stand where we had started. The dog was as perplexed as we were. After a few hours it was time to return to the truck, which the outfitter insisted was to our left.

Fortunately, I have a habit of marking constellations, so I told Spence the outfitter could walk to Alaska if he liked, but we would go the other way, with the North Star at our backs.

The outfitter left, promising to fire a shot when he found the road.

'So what are two guys from Chicago doing unarmed in the Canadian woods in the middle of the night with a crazy outfitter and a wounded and angry bear?' Spence mused.

We stopped after 30 minutes when we heard footsteps crashing through the woods. It was our intrepid outfitter, who had walked into a bog and wisely decided to turn around.

We stood in the silent forest, resigned to stay put until daybreak, when a terrible sound erupted beside us. A pickup truck hurtled past, lights ablaze, 6 feet from where we stood.

We gaped at each other, took two steps and found ourselves on a gravel road. Just 200 yards away rested our pickup truck.

The other time Spence and I got lost was on a dark, bleak night near Separation Lake in Ontario. Again we had tracked a bear and found it deceased when Spence tripped over its body, black bears being especially invisible in the dead of night.

133

We marked the bear with a flag for retrieval the next day and promptly lost our way to the boat. We had no idea where the water was.

Surrounded by 60-foot pines, we could not read the sky. Then I decided we would see a glow from the lights of Dryden, 60 miles south, if someone kindly would climb a tree.

The youngest guy was "volunteered," but all he saw were the Northern Lights, which blanked out everything else.

"So which way are they usually from here?" he was asked.

"North, I suppose," he answered.

So we plowed through hills and gullies in what we thought might be a southerly direction and after an hour we stumbled onto the beach. Our boat was 50 feet away.

We were back in the camp kitchen by 3:30 a.m., gorging on sandwiches and lemonade. And we slept like babies, thinking what fine woodsmen we were.

Of course, where we had gone probably was no more dangerous than being lost in a bathtub, but it took us years to figure that out.

JOHN HUSAR

December 25, 1998

Holiday wishes dear, near to my heart

On Christmas morning I would like to see:
A blanket of fresh snow with huge deer tracks near my cabin.
A friend's wife miraculously cured.
A brother's family at his door.
Double yolks from my chickens.
A crackling hearth, fueled with maple and hickory.
Just enough quiet time to read the grandkids a special story.
My wife's eyes sparkling.
The good luck to smile at the right stranger's face.
A smell of evergreens in the air.
Safety for travelers.
The wisdom to ignite warm, reflective conversation–and to listen.
Cures for diabetes and epilepsy and fibromyalgia.
The chance to visit an old friend's grave.
A call from an Army buddy.
A special warmth in the home of every coach I've ever had.
My editors knowing I forgive them—and hoping they will forgive me.
A family of wild turkeys marching upon my land.

The near-pungent sweetness of freshly roasted walnuts from a grove of trees at the farm.

At least one pot on the stove cooking the wild rice a friend sent from Canada.

A phone call from a fishing buddy saying the ice will be ready soon on a certain lake.

My daughter's book sell a million copies.

A deer sausage just for my 6-year-old granddaughter.

The energy to organize my miserably cluttered bookshelves.

A book of crossword puzzles I can work without screaming.

A football game not smothered by officials (Why can't they learn from soccer referees?).

An end to cheap and dirty politics that wreck renewal of the Cook County forest preserves.

Assurance that Illinois will have its first artificial Lake Michigan reef.

An end to the perch crisis, making thousands of lakefront anglers happy.

Improved access to lakefront harbors for fishermen.

The chance to touch some dear friends that I've missed of late.

Six old broken-down pals from my teen years trying again to harmonize 'Heart of My Heart' on Archer Avenue after 40 years.

A campfire in the snow.

Just one more chance to run a team of spirited Huskies without turning over the sled five or six times.

A week in the Boundary Waters wilderness with two feet of snow on the ground.

Another trip to Canada to watch Spence Petros fish his brains out in horizontally blowing sleet.

Another hairy ride on a tossing boat to rescue Spence at midnight with Babe Winkelman shouting from the helm: 'Watch out for shoals!'

The chance to fulfill a dream of camping six days in the southwestern desert, sleeping by day to watch and hear wildlife by moonlight.

Another camp in the sculptured Flint Hills grasslands of Kansas, shooting quail and prairie chicken by day, mesmerized by tales of settler history and huge stars swirling overhead at night.

Another bike trip across Illinois, riding county blacktops and decent gravel roads, bumming water at farmsteads, reading looks of envy in people's eyes.

Another peek at the Northern Lights.

My first view of the Southern Cross.

A deer stand I can descend without twisting a trick knee.

Two long-lamented fellow college freshmen from Colombia and Costa Rica whom I regretfully failed to bring home for Christmas— and for which I have kicked myself ever since.

A cup of triumphs for the racetrack minister who once took me to the only backstretch living quarters at Sportsman's Park that was decorated with Christmas lights.

A bowl of balm to the Okinawan fishermen who prowled shoreline shallows with their nets one Christmas night, earning a living while our claque of homesick GIs watched from the beach and realized how small our world really was.

Earthly fulfillment for those now-grown children who played with our daughters one bleak holiday night in the crowded Dallas bus station and for their stoic families who made that scene as warm as a certain manger.

Someone to put a flower on my little son's grave a lifetime from here in western Kansas.

Peace and security for that 4-year-old Iraqi girl who was pictured in the Tribune at a bomb site wearing a USA sweatshirt.

And for those of you who waded through all these wistful meanderings, may you have your heart's desire on an always beautiful Christmas Day.

CHAPTER EIGHT

CAMPFIRES

Whether it was Mike Ditka recalling the time he landed a 198-pound marlin or a state conservation police officer talking about nailing a poacher, John could make every person he wrote about sound equally important—and colorful.

Perhaps he was at his best when discussing the pioneer figures who roamed northern Illinois and made it their personal, outdoor habitat and playground, especially Indians. One favorite was Shabbona, the great Pottawatomie chief who was a friend to the area's early white settlers.

John could make it seem as if you were riding in the same canoe with Shabbona as he paddled the Fox River. He loved to look for signs the chief must have used to find his way through the wilderness and retrace trails that have since disappeared.

"I think of the survivalist's tenet that nature doesn't care if you live or die," he wrote. "It just proceeds. Somewhere in the misty floodplains, one can sense buckskin-clad ghosts of another age."

October 30, 1994

The spirit of Shabbona lives in the caves and on the trails

EARLVILLE, Ill.—Les Smith pulled me through the door of his 131-year-old home at Stonehouse Park campground on Indian Creek and jabbed a finger at the arching limb of an ancient oak in his front yard.

"Now isn't that a directional sign?" he demanded. "I know of two other huge old trees like this around here and they all point to the high-ridge trail Chief Shabbona used."

It's known that primitives, including settlers, bent trees with rope ties to give directions. In the North Country, people clipped branches from tall pines to indicate hidden trails.

It's also known that Shabbona himself, the benevolent Pottawatomie chief who tried to warn settlers of the Massacre of 1832, occasionally hunkered in what would be Smith's yard, watching this grand stone house being built. Shabbona's own place was a few miles up the creek in what is now Shabbona State Park.

Although he died in 1859—four years before the lengthy house project was completed and the date '1863' inscribed above the front door-Shabbona has become a central part of the lives of Smith and his family. The enigmatic Indian figures, again and again, in the mystery of the Fox River cave that Smith and his wife, Grace, are trying to decipher.

You may remember my description of a pair of ancient maps—among other historic markings—carved into the wall of this cave in the rocky river bluffs above the town of Wedron. The Smiths had found the cave on a canoe trip and were mesmerized by the carvings. Along with these maps of what turned out to be the Indian Creek drainage system—their creek—the date '1822' was inscribed prominently on a wall.

The Smiths subsequently heard from dozens of people—including historians and descendants of settlers—and now they think they are closer to the truth.

"We probably were right in thinking the cave was used as an outpost by the first surveyors who came here to plat Illinois and Michigan Canal land that was ceded to veterans of the War of 1812," Les said. "But it also was used for much, much more. The fur traders came there, and it probably was a forward supply dump for troops that chased the Indians after the massacre in 1832. There is evidence they had equipment to pull barges across the river from a trail that existed on the other side."

In piecing together fragments of history from local legends and various archives, the Smiths were amazed to learn they were cataloging a previously unknown slice of frontier life. They now have an impressive collection of early maps that locate forgotten forts and expedition routes. Locals have directed them to four more caves that figure in regional history. Three are carved from veins of sand along the Illinois River near Ottawa, which the Smiths think marks the long-lost site of Ft. Ottawa or possibly the little-known Ft. Deposit. Another natural cave lies a mile up Indian Creek from its juncture with the Fox, and it contains some of the same wall markings as the main cave on the Fox.

"This Indian Creek cave probably was a fur trapper's post," Les said. "But the other cave was much more important."

After applying the carvings to new and old maps, Smith believes many other creek systems are indicated, with round gouges marking settlers' homes. "These were maps that told where everyone was" he said. "They even indicate where some people were buried."

Smith has developed an awe for Shabbona, who was a powerful force for settlement. Unlike his contemporaries—Black Hawk, Tecumseh and Waubonsee—Shabbona was peaceful and unusually helpful.

"He was the trail guide, the one you went to if you wanted to go somewhere," Smith said. "He was the Indian who taught settlers how to plant corn. He was the one who grew herbs that healed injuries and cured sicknesses. If you cut yourself with an ax, you went to see him."

"Heck, this Shabbona was a great American who fell out of favor with the Indians because he helped the settlers. If there were justice, that hockey team in Chicago would be called the Shabbonas instead of the Blackhawks, because Black Hawk was a warlike man who sided with the British until the day he died."

Smith has an eerie feeling, wholly unproven, that an 1822 federal agreement with Shabbona might have taken place at this very cave on the Fox. Until then, the Indian Creek system was unknown, not even appearing on the 1818 map of Illinois' first year of statehood.

"This cave was a popular place for Indians," Smith said. "They used it for centuries before the settlers came. There was a major Indian fort nearby." Smith would not be surprised to learn that Shabbona directed, or at least inspired, the carving of the maps himself.

Now that their campground season is over, the Smiths plan a whole winter of studying their caves, camping whenever possible. "Imagine just sitting there at night, thinking of what happened," Les sighed.

Grace said they have been besieged by school groups and local history buffs for tours and glimpses of their homemade video.

"A lot of people around here never realized the richness of their local history," she said. "They never knew so many things happened right around here."

Grinned Les: "It's strange how this has changed our lives. We just were a couple of tent campers who bought an RV park, but what we really bought was part of a museum. It was manifest destiny."

Dec. 14, 1988

At 75, game warden still tracks 'em down

ALBANY, Ill. – Merlin Howe's eyes crinkle when he remembers the angry poacher calling him a crook in court.

The judge's craggy eyebrows rose. "I've known Merlin Howe for years," intoned the magistrate. "And no one calls him a crook in my court. That will be $50 for contempt."

Merlin gave a rasping giggle. "You could have knocked me over with a feather," said the veteran conservation cop. "Why, if I had $50 for every time I've been insulted, I'd be a wealthy man."

Insult, assault, whatever—Merlin has just about seen it all. He has been slugged with paddles and soggy cushions and run over by boats. He has been chased by outlaws in pickup trucks and threatened with guns and hatchets. He has been taunted by the worst backwater, roughneck wildlife thieves and told to beware if he's ever found alone in the wild. His tires have been slit and some calls have been setups.

Yet, for 40 years, Sgt. Merlin Howe has kept hauling them to jail. At 75 and going strong, he is the oldest active game warden in the state, if not in all of America. His district of Whiteside, Lee, Bureau, Henry and Rock Island Counties last year was ranked first among Illinois conservation police.

Although his job is chiefly supervision, it's not unusual for Merlin Howe to make 200 busts himself a year, from something as mundane as fishing without a license to the burglary of ancient Indian graves. He is a nemesis of deer poachers, road hunters, baiters and greedy waterfowl thieves who outshoot their legal limits.

"I guess I just have to know what's going on in a lot of places," he says.

But Merlin Howe also has private interests. Five days a week, he rises at 4:30 a.m. to check the Mississippi River flowing past his door. He makes a few calls to see how the fishing is, then drafts his spots for what is believed to be the oldest continuous radio show in America.

For 39 years, you see, Merlin Howe has been the outdoor voice of WSDR in nearby Sterling. At 6:10 a.m., his is the wise, gentle rumble that greets the morning for countless citizens of northwest Illinois. Station manager Bob Taylor swears that many listeners set their clocks so they can awake to Merlin's fishing and hunting reports.

Now and then, Howe takes on multibillion-dollar corporations. Fifteen years ago, he investigated and filed pollution charges as a private citizen against Commonwealth Edison Company's Cordova nuclear plant and a nearby 3-M plant on the Mississippi River, winning substantial fines and concessions.

"I kept the state out of it," Howe explained. "By doing it on my own time, I was able to do exactly what I wanted."

He also has nailed three railroads on pollution charges and currently wages a one-man vendetta against careless fleeting methods by the barge industry on the Mississippi River.

For 20 years, Howe has seethed as barges have been illegally tied to trees on a federal wildlife refuge in the river. Fortunately for the barge companies, the refuge is on an island on the Iowa side and Howe is legally powerless to do much more than raise Cain with the U.S. Fish and Wildlife Service, the U.S. Coast Guard and the U.S. Army Corps of Engineers.

He has collected hundreds of photos, attended dozens of meetings and generally been as thorny as possible toward an industry that he contends wantonly rips trees from refuges by tying, then abandoning, heavy barges.

"We used to have heron rookeries here, but not anymore," Howe says, pointing toward a string of barges tied to 3-mile-long Beaver Island, just across the river from his house.

To big and small outdoor miscreants throughout northwest Illinois,

Merlin Howe is everywhere, or can be, or might be. If not now, then later.

He is proud of the fact that he has eight families who are regulars. I've been getting them for three generations. One family now is in its fourth. I've nailed the grandfather, the father and mother, the sons– and now the son's son. I know most of 'em so well that they invite me to dinner when I go out to their places on an investigation. They say: "Hi, Merlin, whatcha lookin' for now? But first have a bite to eat."

Trim and fit from walking seven miles at a crack, Howe carries a homemade wooden 'shotgun' to make himself appear as a hunter. This can let him get close enough to peer into a suspect's bag before any evidence can be tossed away. He spends hours parked on rural lanes late at night, watching for the illegal spotlights of deer and raccoon poachers.

"Every time I catch one, they always say they're looking for a lost dog," Howe says with a laugh. "I just tell 'em that their dog must have squirrel blood."

He remembers warmly the old days of 'river rats' and justice of the peace courts, when violators were guilty unless proven innocent.

"You've got to remember that these JPs were paid $4 or $5 for every case and they knew that no officer was going to bring people to them if a lot were going to be found innocent," Howe mused. "There was one judge who gave 'em two choices: Plead guilty or go to jail. Some of those JP courts were something else. One judge was a cook in a restaurant. The subjects sat at stools while he stood behind the counter holding a spatula."

Howe said he used to "look down on river rats, those old guys who lived in shanties and just trapped, hunted and fished. But I learned to respect them. They were our first real resource people, because they never took too much. They always left some fish and wildlife to breed for next year.

"They were incredible people who took their water straight from the river, but never got sick. They'd make coffee, but the only time they'd clean the pot was when the grounds got so thick you couldn't add any water. They never cleaned their frying pans. They'd just wait until their pan got too gummed up, then they'd buy a new pan. We don't have river rats today. Not like them. What we have I'd call river mice."

Howe's most heroic moment occurred during the Mississippi River floods of 1965, when he was trapped in Fulton for 22 days with the only two-way radio in town. His Civil Defense efforts led to a rare commendation by the Illinois General Assembly.

Howe intends to keep on working—and patrolling—as long as he can. "I don't drive as fast any more and I don't run down muddy, rocky levees and I don't cross creeks on a limb any more, either," he said. "But I still get that surge when I get a good one. When I get to the point where I don't get a thrill out of catching a poacher, then I'll give it up."

JOHN HUSAR

December 1, 1985

Poachers can't trap a legend

LELAND, Ill.—"Poacher" is a dirty word to Phil Cole, especially when the poacher is a cop.

In his 15 years as a state conservation police officer, the laconic ex-Aurora barber has nailed four fellow policemen for violating game laws.

In several cop houses around northern Illinois—and especially in Sheridan, Streator, Henry and Colona—Cole's name has been anathema. In others, though, it is spoken in tones of awe.

That's because he not only arrested the policemen for poaching raccoons or deer on duty, but, following the letter of the law, he confiscated their patrol cars as well as their guns.

The towns did get back the squad cars after lengthy delays. But not until three of those cops were fired and the other was suspended without pay for a month. And the state disposed of the guns.

"To an awful lot of small-town cops out here, Phil Cole is a living legend," said James 'Bud' Harton, a former Chicago railroad detective who now wears a police badge in tiny Leland, near the northern border of La Salle County.

"I'm not easily impressed by police officers, but Phil Cole—he's in another class. Phil's reputation is incredible."

Cole is more than a rigid enforcer of game laws whose latest coup is the arrest of a farmer and impoundment of his combine and two guns for shooting protected hen pheasants while harvesting corn. He also is hell on wheels when it comes to red-light-and-siren, *Dukes of Hazzard*–type chases over the rural roads.

"I don't know what he's done to his car, but he has passed me at 100 miles an hour, one arm lazily resting on the top of the seat," Harton said.

"He's so good at pursuit that most of the dispatchers now call him if he's in the area when there's any kind of chase or emergency, because they know he'll probably get there first"

How fast does he push his Dodge Ram Charger?

"I dunno," Cole says in an embarrassed half-mumble. "I arrested one guy this summer going 120 miles per hour, and I was going pretty much all-out. He was on a motorcycle."

Cole's eyes twinkle when you ask if he has souped up his state vehicle.

"Nope," he says. "Can't. Policy says you can't alter a thing." And then he smiles.

Cole is a steely eyed, slender, 41-year-old 'cowboy' who wears a low-slung holster and camo jackets. His territory includes La Salle and parts of Lee and Whiteside Counties, but like the Lone Ranger, he goes wherever needed. His superiors call him a 'dedicated' cop, one of the best in the state.

"I wouldn't want to be anything but a conservation cop," Cole said, although his friends keep asking him to run for sheriff. "It's probably the best job there is, considering the versatility, the outdoors, the people, the good you can do for the resource." His main frustration stems from a court ruling that strictly limits officers to eight-hour days—an impossible time frame when one guns for poachers who operate night and day.

"That 40-hour-a-week policy is really a handicap for us, because it means there's a lot of time when we can't be on the air," Cole said. "Honestly, I probably work 14 hours a day, but I don't put 14 hours down."

Cole is known for his diligence, once taking 10 days to catch a notorious poacher who threatened a hunter who had seen him shoot a deer. "It took me one day just to back-trail him from his stand to see where he went out," Cole said, "and four more days to find where he lived."

Cole first arrested a policeman 12 years ago, an acquaintance who had been shining and shooting 'coons out of season. The officer's Sheridan squad car was parked outside town while he and a friend hunted in the friend's pickup truck.

"I was following 'em without lights—Jeez, don't put that in—when he was dropped off at the police car," Cole said. "I never did get the other guy. Didn't really want to. I had what I wanted."

Five years ago in Streator, Cole tracked down an officer after a citizen had reported seeing a deer shot from a police car. In Henry, he gave an officer a warning when he found him shining deer at night.

"He told me he was looking for cattle on the road," Cole said. "An hour-and-a-half later, he was back out shining with a loaded rifle in his car. It was obvious to me what he was doing." This time the policeman was arrested.

Cole last year assisted fellow officer Jim Thomas in the arrest and conviction of a Colona policeman for poaching deer with a rifle. Cole's friends say his goal is to nail 10 cops before he retires in five more years.

"Policemen can be really bad when they think they're above the law" explained Harton.

Cole said he usually surprises traffic or criminal offenders when they discover they've been stopped by a conservation cop.

"Most people think of us as 'game wardens,' when we actually have full police powers,"he said. "We're trained the same as state troopers, except we're paid a lot less."

Cole doesn't think it's out of the ordinary for conservation cops to pitch in when necessary.

"You have to do that in a rural area, because there aren't that many of us out here," he said. "I certainly don't enjoy the high-speed chases. They're dangerous. But you can't say no if someone needs help. And I'm not going to let a drunk drive down the road and maybe kill someone in another mile."

JOHN HUSAR

February 18, 1996

14-year-old video star fishing's new wave

"See the girl in the back booth with the fishing hat? Tall kid, willowy. Strong, determined eyes. Confident mouth. She's 14, but looks more like 16. The one with the long-sleeved fishing shirt with enough sponsors' patches to rival an Indy car driver."

I gave a shove to Kenny Schneider's arm.

"Go over there and ask her a fishing question," I urged. "Give her a little test."

Playing along, Schneider—who is one of Chicago's more competent fishermen—sidled to the booth where Michelle Fitch sat at the Tinley Park Outdoor Show. She was hawking guide trips for her mentor on Shabbona Lake and, incidentally, selling an instructional video. Her video. The one she made with veteran guide Roger Davis.

"So what's the best bait for trophy bass?" Schneider asked as casually as possible.

Fitch didn't blink an eye.

"Jig and pig," came the answer.

"So what's the best overall bass lure?" Schneider persisted.

"Plastic worm," was Fitch's response.

Schneider reeled back through the aisle.

"How old did you say she was? Fourteen?" he said. "Well, she isn't supposed to know stuff like that yet. This kid's going to be phenomenal."

The world is on the verge of discovering just how far this honors freshman at Lincoln-Way High School East might go in a fishing world still relatively untouched by women. She hopes to be a full-fledged fishing guide in two more years—as soon as she's old enough to run a boat for hire.

Davis, a DeKalb County sheriff's lieutenant who has guided at Shabbona since 1990, remembers his first encounter with Fitch when she was 12.

"Her father had booked a half-day trip with me for her birthday," he said. "We were to meet around 11 a.m., but they'd been out there since the lake opened at 6 a.m., fishing the shoreline. I figured this was going to be a disaster. The kid would be burned out by 2 o'clock, squirming in the boat, whining to go home. I expected the worst."

What he got was a vacuum cleaner of fishing information—a hungry companion who absorbed everything he could teach. Fitch drained him with questions, stunned him with her quick read of his methods. She not only had the touch to "feel" and catch fish, but she quickly advanced into sophisticated areas. By evening, well after the trip was scheduled to end, Fitch had caught her first bass on artificial bait—a

4-pounder—and lost one she swears was 2 pounds heavier. She still gives that fish a determined shot on each trip to Shabbona Lake.

"We finally quit around 9:30 or so, and if there had been any light she still would have gone on," Davis said. "I couldn't believe her. Fourteen hours on the water and she still wanted more."

The Fitches booked one more trip with Davis that summer, and he had seen enough. He told the Fitches they could fish with him whenever they wanted, just like friends. No charge. They would buy the bait, he would provide the gas.

"What I think happened was that Roger found someone who liked fishing as much as he does, and for the very same reasons," said Michelle's father, Mike Fitch, a manager at Acme Steel in Riverdale. "I think that was the instant chemistry."

Each time they fished with Davis, Fitch behaved more and more like a pro. She reached the point where she would bomb away in Davis' boat, while her father fished by himself.

"I couldn't keep up with them," her dad said. "Theirs was a different level of intensity. My idea of fishing was to start on one side of the lake, put out a couple of lines at different depths, then sit back and let the wind drift me across the lake. Not Michelle. She couldn't stand that. She'd be switching baits, switching colors. She'd give a spot 10 minutes, then want to zoom away. She was constantly playing wind, sun, the color of water. I'd just want to sit there and wait for the fish to come along. I'd stay with the same bait all day long."

With one video on bass fishing under his belt, Davis wanted to create another that emphasized the art of using live bait on Shabbona.

"This can be a tough lake to fish, but if you know how to select the right bait and methods for different species, you can do pretty well," he explained.

"And since I needed a partner for the video, I couldn't think of anyone more suitable than Michelle."

At first the youngster was stunned by the idea. Having at least two dozen fishing videos in her collection, she had some idea of the expertise it would take. But Davis and her father encouraged her, and last year they put together *Live Bait Techniques on Shabbona Lake,* which turned out to be a better-than-average instructional video, with Fitch carrying her weight as well as Davis expected.

Fitch learned to fish for bluegill and bullhead in a small pond behind the family's Mokena home, and her father could see she had talent.

"Before long, she was casting all the way across the pond," he said.

When she was 10, the family took a day trip to Shabbona, rented a boat and caught some fish. They didn't go back again until Michelle insisted on that guided trip for her 12th birthday. A year ago she wrote a 15-page research paper on the history and techniques of bass fishing that rivals anything published in local outdoor magazines.

Now she sits in booths, fielding questions with aplomb, enjoying the discomfiture of those who can't believe she knows what she knows.

"I can see it's not easy for some of these men," she said. "They're three times my age and I'm a kid answering their questions. Sometimes they go over and ask Roger the same questions. It's hard for them to handle the fact that I'm a girl and I'm intelligent enough to be doing this."

Her school friends are equally disconcerted.

"They make fun of me," Fitch conceded. "The guys don't think I should be doing this, and the girls can't believe I'll spend whole weekends at fishing expos."

For a while friends joshed her, calling her "Fishstix." But she liked the nickname and now has it sewn on her official shirts.

"As far as I'm concerned, she's my partner," Davis said. "When a sponsor sends me a shirt, they send her one too. She gets the same rods, reels and other equipment."

Fitch now has five shirts, a jacket, 20 rods and 25 reels. And 10 tackle boxes full of fishing lures.

And, above all, her very own, well-received, fishing video.

JOHN HUSAR

May 7, 1985

Fisherman Ditka's catch: No salmon, lots of sleep

Mike Ditka stared across the deep green waves, then looked away. It was not his kind of day.

If the Bear coach had wanted green, he'd be on a golf course threatening his handicap of 6, not chasing salmon around Lake Michigan to humor corporate executives paying incredible money to bask amid celebrity.

But this, of course, was an exception. The payment was $10,000 and the beneficiary was cancer research. Imagine that—$10,000 to fish for six hours with the steeltown kid from Aliquippa, Pa. Ditka willingly bobbed along.

There were others who rode Monday's crests with utter bemusement in Bill Cullerton's All-Star Sportfishing tournament.

Joey Meyer, the De Paul coach, remembered when $10,000 would have been a nifty yearly income for an assistant coach. Stash Mikita, as adept on water as he was on ice, could imagine 10 grand feeding his old neighborhood back in Czechoslovakia. Babe Winkelman, the TV fishing star, starved for years to pursue his dream. There were times when he could've killed for $10,000.

And now this was the price for weighing sinkers with them. It's a funny world.

Fortunately, Monday was a spectacular day on the lakefront. From a calm morning palette of gray-blue-green pastels to brilliant afternoon sunshine in a light chop, the day was made for fishing and Ditka was surrounded by talent. There was Joe Cottini, skipper of the "Tammy

153

Ann," veteran of herring times on the lake, of bass and bluegill and crappie in the salad days of Lincoln Park lagoon, 12 years a charter captain. There was Don Mahlstedt of Deerfield, who once cranked a marlin for 3 hours 25 minutes, spooling a 650-yard reel six times until his arms went numb.

"I couldn't do that," Ditka said. "I once spent a little over an hour to boat a 198-pound marlin in Mazatlan, Mexico, and that was enough."

The thought occurred that Ditka's fish was about the size of a man.

"Hmph," he said admiringly. "Most men wouldn't fight for an hour. They'd give up."

Fighting is more in tune with Ditka's style than the gentle pathways of nature.

"My dad never raised me with hunting and fishing," he said. "Not in a steel-mill town. I've never gone bass fishing or anything like that."

But pro sports creates strange bedfellows, and Ditka has availed himself of some unique opportunities.

He once found himself off Freeport, the Bahamas, tying into a school of dolphins with some fellow players. His arms had never been so tired.

"And grouper. Reeling in a grouper is like pulling a piece of lead off the bottom," he said.

Ditka allowed that once in a while is enough. "They tell me about 600-pound marlin off Hawaii, of fighting them for 10 hours," he said. "That's nonsense. Why, that's two rounds of golf right there."

Ditka played two rounds—sans two holes—on Sunday, and regretted the darkness that cost him those two holes.

Now he was staring deckward through the Tammy Ann's hatch where his partners anxiously awaited a fish to strike one of eight lures trolling half a mile off 31st Street.

"To me, going out for two, three, four hours to catch three or four fish is, well, it don't mean a lot to me," Ditka said, his eyes growing leaden.

It meant so little, in fact, that he yielded all but his first turn at a fish to nap below.

He stirred at the idea of shooting birds now and then. "In Texas, I shot some doves, which was kinda interesting, and some quail. Also at a shooting preserve out on Route 173, where Walter (Payton) and (Roland) Harper go.

"I also went out with the Dallas guys once to that huge ranch near Uvalde, Tex., owned by the former governor, Dolph Briscoe. It's the second biggest ranch in Texas, right behind the King Ranch, and they let us shoot anything—birds, snakes, javelinas, coyotes, rabbits. We could've shot deer, but we didn't because they were out of season. But he had thousands and thousands of deer there. We had pistols, rifles, shotguns, and we rode in the back of trucks."

Ditka emerged for the noon radio report, which for our boat wasn't encouraging. We had gambled on kings in the shallows off the South Side, when all the action turned out to 110 feet out northwest of the Loop, generally at 35 to 50 feet.

"Tell 'em we caught a 200-pound sturgeon," Ditka barked, then went back below.

He awoke again an hour before lines were to come out, our total a miserable six fish—one 8-pound chinook, two rainbows and three small coho. "This is great," Ditka needled. "I was assured we'd be catching 15, 20 fish. You guys must have negative attitudes."

Don Rosuck of Highland Park, president of Culligan International Co., sponsor of the boat, kidded that Ditka's beauty sleep was to blame.

"Three times we let your fish swim away out there," Rosuck said."It kept hollering, 'Mike, Mike, come out!' but you wouldn't listen."

"I guess I'll be a fisherman when I get to that Great Pond in the Sky," Ditka allowed.

At the dock, however, Ditka revealed a proper soul for fishing. One of the photographers insisted on knowing how many fish he caught.

Ditka showed little resistance. "Two," he lied, raising a pair of fingers.

He'll be a fisherman yet.

CHAPTER NINE
OVERNIGHTERS

At a big newspaper like the Chicago Tribune, *there is an informal fantasy game played every day at more than a few desks, especially after a particularly trying day of wrestling with copy or sources or both. It goes something like this: If you could have any job at the newspaper, what would it be? What would you do? What beat would you cover?*

Frequently during the 1980s and 1990s at the Tribune, the answer to the what-if question would be to covet John Husar's job as outdoors writer and columnist. It seemed only too wonderful and exciting to be paid for being outdoors in nature.

While John championed the nature in the Midwest, including his "own corner of the Cook County woods" as he called it, his job as a big-city outdoors writer included travel to exotic and remote places (sometimes the emphasis was more on the latter, other times the former).

We all envied him for those trips—and fantasized in awe at his reports.

JOHN HUSAR

September 15, 1988

Torch-carrying honor lights up his emotions

INCHON, South Korea—I was told this would be a hard story to write. That too much emotion is compressed into the thousands of impressions that fly through a person's mind while carrying the Olympic torch.

That may be correct.

I had imagined that I would dwell upon the part I'd play in carrying on a precious tradition. Years ago, as a little kid, I'd sometimes trot through a South Side Chicago alley with a weak flame flickering from a stick. I don't know why, but my young mind had equated the torch run with winning a marathon. There was something inexpressibly glorious in the notion of bearing a lighted torch.

I finally saw the real thing in 1980 from a window of the high school in Lake Placid, N.Y., when the flame came to the Winter Olympics. I remember musing on how far that flame had traveled and the many things it represents to different people.

In time, there were other flames, in Sarajevo, Los Angeles and Calgary. I was always struck by the pride and joy on the faces of those torch bearers, especially the ones who bore the flame from wheelchairs. I could understand the honor of being part of something as stirring as the Olympics.

I thought I had understood, that is, until my own turn came Wednesday evening in the dusky air of South Korea's industrial port city of Inchon. Halfway around the globe from home in an emerging Third World nation, I would be one of 30 foreign journalists—only six from the United States—invited to participate in South Korea's euphoric expression of new-found stature in the world community.

And, suddenly, I was as nervous as a cat.

My assignment was on relay section No. 1408, in the Nam Dong dis-

158

trict of Inchon, which had not been favored with world-class attention since General MacArthur's surprise landing led to the recapture of Seoul in late 1950. I would bear the torch for 1.2 kilometers amid six broad traffic lanes on Jang Su Street, from the Min Jung Dang Sa police building to the five-pronged Kansug O Kory intersection leading to City Hall. I would be one of 1,539 torch carriers in Korea.

Many others would run, of course. A total of 20,946 had been given a place on the route, but most were to be in double lines of escorts accompanying the torch. I met my 16 escorts two hours before our run in the local civil defense building, where we changed into our uniform shorts and tank tops and were issued our headbands and formal white gloves.

We were shown how to stand in twin lines facing forward when the torch arrived. A secondary runner, sort of a lieutenant, would bark orders for the ceremony. At his commands, new and old torch bearers would turn toward each other, pass the flame and pivot back. Then the new runners would begin their leg of the journey. Anxious officials drilled me on where to stand and what to do to avoid ruining an Asian ceremony that clearly meant much to them.

An hour before the flame came, we went to the street. Thousands of people already had lined the curbs. We posed for many, many pictures while a marching band of folk percussionists made the air pulse with the throbbing rhythm of drums.

With half an hour to go, a van arrived with my torch. I examined the polished copper and cloisonned engravings of a pair of fire-belching dragons. The other runners craned to see, and so I offered each the torch. The men at first were surprised, but one by one they took it and held it aloft. Some officious bureaucrats were not certain that this should be done—it certainly was not in the script—and tried to steer me away. But I informed them as nicely as possible that every man in this group was going to touch that torch. Nearby a nervous young woman was splendidly dressed in a full-length Korean formal gown. She was there to drape a garland of flowers around my neck. She seemed jarred when she, too, was given the torch.

Several other women then asked for a turn, and I later moved along the crowd at the curb, presenting the torch to children and adults.

People lined up to pose for pictures, grinning hugely when they received the torch. Children were thrust forward by parents for photographic proof that they had been on hand when their Korea received the symbolic respect of the world.

That, I think, is what the flame meant to many of them. After 3,000 years of steady oppression, a new stature was enveloping a little country that had seen only a history of invasion. Through the Olympic flame, the world was assuring them that Korea had been elevated to an exclusive circle. No people could have behaved more proudly.

Then the flashing lights of police cars turned the corner, followed by trucks of photographers, a busful of soldiers, more vans and a phalanx of motorcycle cops. The drums pulsated, and the people caught their breath as the flame danced into sight.

I faced the proper way, and then the flame was beside me. The young lady draped me with her flowers. The command barked: "Ja-u, yung-wu!" and four columns of runners pivoted to face each other. Drums and firecrackers and the cheers of people made it hard to hear the call to touch torches. My Korean counterpart caught my eyes and smiled as we made the exchange.

I dimly heard the order to turn forward, and then began a slow trot as the vehicles eased ahead.

For weeks, I had wondered what I would think and how I would conduct my run. Now I was running in a blur, vaguely aware of a screaming, waving crowd. I concentrated on the yellow center line. An official in a car ahead motioned for me to wave the torch at the crowd, to smile and enjoy the moment, and that's when I knew what I would do.

Each wave then became a symbol for someone dear, for Mom and Dad and the family, for Louise and the girls, for other runners on my newspaper team who equally deserved to be where I was now—Phil and Skip and Bob and Steve—and for the colleagues back in Chicago—Bernie and Rico and Linda and Julie and the others—plus the multitude of other journalists who should cover their own Olympics someday. And for the guys who ran with me when we were kids.

I noticed that hardly anyone was watching me, that most eyes were on the sacred flame. I'd wave the torch and people would scream and wave back, sometimes hundreds at a time, little girls in colored formals, boys in school ties and Boy Scout uniforms. Young adults and even cops waved at the flame.

I found myself trying to make eye contact, savoring the astonishment when people sensed a personal salute from the bearer of the sacred flame. Before long, dozens of young people were running behind the crowds, keeping pace with the flame, hurrying toward the next exchange.

Too soon, the run was over. We halted beside another double column of runners, this one including women, obeyed the commands, passed the flame and then watched another torch lumber toward City Hall.

But we weren't through. The people came out to greet us, to touch our hands, to present their children. Another round of photos began.

Later, at a reception on the second floor of a bulgogi restaurant, the four relay teams from Nam Dong district sat barefoot and crosslegged at long tables, toasting each other with spirits and beer. We clapped to the rhythm of each other's songs. Mine was the Kansas alma mater.

One of the woman runners was moved by my flushed cheeks and vigorously fanned me to cool down. Her intentions were charitable, but she couldn't have known that my slick of sweat was not from running too hard or too long.

Mine was the pure excitement of a thrilled and pounding heart.

June 25, 1995

A cabin, a swing and communing with owls

FRANKLIN GROVE, Illinois—The old double-rutted gravel road is overgrown with what some folks think are common weeds now, but others know better. Those are the mystic companions of a creekside summer, the nettles and their antidotes, the Touch-Me-Nots, flourishing side by side.

The nettles will leave you in blistered, stinging agony should you be foolish enough to wear shorts or T-shirts in their damp woodland company. But all you have to do is find the round-lobed Touch-Me-Nots, also known as jewelweed, that almost always share the turf. Their fat, juicy stems are translucent. Squeeze one and the luscious sap bubbles inside like soda in a plastic straw. Break it open and smear that viscous juice upon the red, raw nettle scrapes. The pain subsides just like that.

Elmer Stauffer, who runs a little-known wild plant paradise called Franklin Creek State Park, says Touch-Me-Nots also will ward off the agonies of poison ivy. If so, I won't willingly test it. Not that I don't have all the chances in the world. These beautiful prairie groves of north-central Illinois are stuffed with poison ivy in every deceptive shape. Only heaven knows how many substantially different leaves on vines and various shrub-like growths can turn out to be poison ivy.

Yet so far I've escaped its ravages. I must be one of those lucky folks blessed with immunity. I've practically lived in poison ivy. I've lunched on it, napped in it, hunted deer against it, even jogged and ridden bikes right into it—even after I got good at recognizing what it was. So far, never a rash. Nothing but innocent bliss. Knock on wood. But I've learned to keep an eye peeled for patches of Touch-Me-Nots. You never know. Besides, I do have this magnetism for nettles.

And mosquitoes. I wish I could find a plant whose crushed leaves did the job on mosquitoes. Now that spring's floods have subsided, the bottomlands of every creek in Illinois are abuzz with hungry, angry, overheated insects. I try to avoid most of those common sprays loaded with absorbent poisons so strong they can melt plastic. The best alternate I can find is one of those pricey bug jackets from the better outdoor stores, the kind made of mesh covered by mosquito netting. The mesh holds the netting so far above the skin that no mosquito's stinger can reach far enough to do its nasty work.

I've used them for two years on bear hunts in the bug-ridden Canadian wilds. Now I wear one on my cabin's swing. And sometimes with a head net. Thank heaven for hunting gear.

The bug jacket and head net also make for excellent camouflage. The other night I sat above an insect-humming pond within 30 yards of two owls, a pair of beavers, a roosting heron, a foraging red fox, a groundhog in a tree and three deer, none of which knew I was there. Even with my smelly cigar.

The owls like to perch on the hillside in tall sugar maples, which leaves them halfway up the tree but eye-level with my swing. We face each other and make owl talk, which lately involves a nervous whistling hiss. I must be getting good at it. Whenever I try to hiss like an owl, the chipmunks beside the cabin dive for cover into a rockpile.

We all hissed as the red fox poked around the pond, perhaps hunting frogs. But the fox merely waved us off with his tail.

The tree-climbing groundhog never looked up. My wife and I thought he was dead, his immobile bulk slung loosely over a branch. Could he possibly have been deposited there by a brawny owl whose eyes were too big for its stomach? Then the groundhog woke up, yawned, stretched and clambered down the tree. I've never seen that before.

Meanwhile, the beavers were busily making waves and—as it turned out—babies. We now have at least one 12-inch-long youngster skirting the bluegill beds in the pond, slapping at nothing with its tiny tail.

For a while this spring, everyone got a little nasty. The owls would hiss when I'd go outside at night to walk the dog. Once I arrived at the cabin late at night and parked beneath an owl tree. I was hissed all the way to the door.

The deer, too, have been taking liberties. They think nothing of sneaking toward the campfire and jumping fences behind our backs. Then they hang around in the darkness, snorting and stomping and carrying on until we yield the night and go inside to bed.

This was a good spring on Franklin Creek. The thick carpets of bluebells lasted over a month. And now that the stream's at a normal level, the fish have begun to bite. Dark, sweet mulberries already droop low, filling your palm with the brush of a hand. And the bull-frogs have just begun their nightly banjo concerts.

Best of all, near the nettles we see blossoms on other thorny appendages. Yep, the wet spring has promised an overwhelming raspberry crop.

And you know the antidote for that. Come late June and early July, brew a pot of coffee and pop a thick pie into the oven. After baking, when it cools, spoon on maybe a quart of yogurt or ice cream.

June 23, 1986

Seals, walruses an accompaniment to Arctic night

IGLOOLIK, Canada—After a while, the sled was packed with camping gear, a box of food, a few extra jugs of snowmobile fuel and eight thick caribou hides.

Tribune colleague Stan Cook and I pounced upon the stack of hides and leaned back. Emile Immaroituk, Eskimo hunter and scholar, took a final whack at an oily rib of seal from a pot in his little kitchen on the edge of the Melville Peninsula in Canada's Northwest Territories. He stooped through his low front door, kicked the snowmobile to life and we were off, tethered by a 10-foot rope.

This would be our first taste of a sun-bright arctic night. On other stops of this 20-day journalistic tour, we would encounter polar bears and musk oxen, arctic fox and wolves. Now we were foraying to the icy home of ringed seals and walruses.

The tiny Eskimo hamlet of Igloolik, its seal hides stretched on frames beside nearly every window, disappeared behind a hill. We crossed a pair of small, rocky islands and slipped onto the fairly smooth pack ice of Hecla and Fury Strait, named for explorer Edward Parry's ships.

From time to time, we encountered other sleds of hunting parties and we'd stop to chat. Emile would note the seal or caribou carcasses and check the condition of the trail ahead. We soon were aware of a network of arctic travelers casually keeping tabs on one another. In this way, everyone comes to know where each has been and where they are headed and what they might expect to find.

We were alone, but not really. There is comfort and protection in a word- of-mouth trail, the only kind that you can leave in the vast expanse of the arctic. Especially if something should happen and someone might want to look for you.

Emile showed us how to find the black, distant commas of seals sunning on the ice. Once in a while we'd chase one, gunning the snowmobile toward the sleeping outline. It would pick up our vibrations within a hundred yards or so, squint once and dive through the hole in the five- to six-foot crust of ice. Sometimes we'd see five or 10 seals in an hour.

We stopped once beside three sealskin-clad families having tea. They were heading for a hunt on an open water flowage and were resting beside their sleds. We shared their tea and bannock, patted their dogs and watched their youngsters play stickball on the ice.

Emile's plan was to camp on the mouth of a passage between Baffin and Jens Munk islands, within sight of the sheer cliffs of Baffin's bulk. That would put us some 17 miles from an open flowage where walruses spend the winter.

"We must not camp too close or we might scare them away," Emile explained. "We must hope that no one comes to hunt them from the other direction." That would be from Pond Inlet, more than 150 miles away but just two days' travel for the modern Eskimo.

Our green-domed tent was large enough for four, leaving plenty of room to drape clothes inside. We stomped the snow to smooth out bumps and spread the warm caribou skins across the floor. The sleeping bags went on top. A Coleman stove gave us supper and heat. Our snow knife provided an endless supply of water. We were snug and warm.

Emile is a storied guide employed by his local government to teach young Eskimos the old ways of finding game. He travels by reading patterns carved by the prevailing winds in old snow. In this way, he finds direction even in whiteouts, when the overcast sky and snow blend so perfectly that one is left with no sense of space.

He is a link to the Eskimos' nomadic past, a grandson of the last king of Igloolik whose family weathered the periodic ravages of starvation. He is a drum dancer of awesome reputation, destined to spend the month of August at Expo in Vancouver to demonstrate that story-telling talent. He has spent the last four years compiling a dictionary of his native language.

That night, with the midnight sun shining through our green tent, Emile stirred his cup of tea and described the privations of his people.

"My grandmother survived a time when the people starved," he said slowly. She was married then the first time, and they were camped in September or October at a time when no animals would come, and everyone was sick.

"Her husband was dying, and he told her again and again that she would eat him when he died. "No," she said. "I mate you. I no eat you." But he always answered that she would.

"In time, he died and only she and one old woman were left. They tried to remove his body from the bed, but they were too weak. The other woman looked at my grandmother and reminded her of what her husband had said. "He said that you would eat him, and now you will."

"My grandmother cried and tried again to move his body, but she could not. So they took out their knives and began to cut his body and they ate him. My grandmother cried and cried, and then the other woman died, and so my grandmother ate her, too.

"When the spring came, she was alone and there, of course, was no more food. It was May and she looked outside the igloo and saw in the distance a tiny movement of a dog team. It came closer—a man and a wife and a little girl on their way to Pond Inlet from Igloolik. They saw her come out of the ice house looking like a bird—a long neck and long, thin legs. She couldn't walk, she was so weak. And they took her back to Igloolik, and there she met my grandfather, and that is how I came to be."

He stirred another cup of tea. Yes, he said, they possibly had camped somewhere right around here.

The morning was purplish gray. Five seals were on the ice within a two-mile radius of our tent.

My breakfast of oatmeal raisin granola did nothing for Emile, and we went in search of his staple of fresh meat. We found the open water a mile off the coast of Baffin, traversing a number of ominous cracks. We crept afoot the last half-mile, but the brown-skinned walruses had seen us and slipped off their shelf of ice.

They watched from 80 yards away in the water as we inspected their crusty, body-heated beds. The snow was stained thoroughly by their mess. They slipped farther along the ice edge, then dove and were gone. We returned to the sled when Emile beckoned. "We will see if they move a little farther," he said, and he was right. They had slipped into a tiny bay perhaps 200 yards away.

We motored over, cut the engine and sat like stones. The walruses rose and watched us, then dove again. We rode a little farther. Emile broke out the stove, cut some snow and began to make tea. Five minutes later, seven walruses broke the surface no more than 25 yards away.

We stared and they looked back. They swam for another hour out there—five adults, including a huge male, plus a couple of youngsters. Emile unwrapped the hind half of a frozen arctic char and sliced off some bite-sized morsels and rubbed his ailing stomach.

"Good, good," he murmured when we accepted the orange flesh. The cool, smooth texture agreeably had no more than a vague fishiness. We thought of how a snack like that would cost a fortune in some sushi bar back home.

In time we packed up and moved toward the tiny island called Jens Munk, once probably a part of Baffin. The caribou would be there, Emile believed, and we slowly wound our way around the low, rocky hills, eyes peeled for fresh tracks in the snow.

We had gone six miles into a biting wind when we discovered a camera case missing. Without a word, Emile retraced the route and, six miles back, drove to the half-buried bag among some rugged ice. The detour proved a blessing, for we soon encountered four young caribou grazing in the thin snow atop a hill. Emile cut the engine and we sat perfectly still.

We inched forward over the next hour, 20 to 25 yards at a time. We'd stop when a reindeer would raise its head. We'd wait until they all began to graze again. We'd wait an extra five or 10 minutes, then start the engine and creep ahead some more.

We were 125 yards away when Emile tugged his rusty old Remington .223 from the cushion of his seat. He dismounted and crept on foot, pausing, patiently waiting, then gaining another step.

He finally selected a young doe and missed high. Two animals turned their heads as the bullet spat up a distant film of snow.

He aimed lower and missed, then aimed even lower and missed once more. The animals turned to face us but did not flee. He finally found his mark and dropped the doe, and we hurried to make sure it couldn't get away.

We had it on the sled before the others were out of sight. Later in camp, Emile would have it perfectly skinned and butchered in 17 minutes.

The next day, we skirted the other flowage and found five hunters with a quartet of seals. They stood on sleds beside the open water, awaiting the migrating mammals. Now and then one would pop up its head within a hundred yards and a shot would ring and the hunter would paddle forth in a leaky wooden boat to retrieve his prey.

The precious skins were folded inside-out. Then the carcasses would be dressed and the livers devoured. Emile quickly helped himself to several huge slices of raw seal liver, possibly the most popular native food throughout the north.

"Ahh," he smiled, patting his happy tummy. Two weeks later, we would try some raw seal liver, too, requiring the experience. And it would be wonderful–a fine, smooth texture. A delicate aroma of shucked oysters. Very few outsiders can express that, since very few hungry seal hunters make it home with much liver left.

The night before, we had indulged in shoulder of caribou. Emile boiled it 25 minutes in a pot of Lipton's chicken noodle soup, and the meaty chunks were excellent.

He had found the tent that day in a virtual whiteout, and we had not been worried in the least. He had used the old navigator's trick of purposely missing wide. Just estimate the distance needed to travel, turn when you think it's right, and two miles later run straight into the tent-gray instead of green in the blowing snow. Nothing to it at all.

There were more Eskimo stories that evening—of families lost on floes, of great hunts and great dogs and of a great people who once wandered purposely through endless winter snows. Of a people now settled but struggling to relearn some of the old ways.

And two more seals greeted us in the morning outside our tent.

JOHN HUSAR

August 25, 1997

Fishing at the edge of the earth

CORDOVA, Alaska—Our single-engine Otter rose from a rain-puddled tarmac into the aftermath of another brutal Alaskan storm.

In certain corners of Prince William Sound, 16-foot waves beat upon the shoreline. On the Gulf of Alaska, remote campers near the mouth of the Tsiu River were in their fourth day of being stranded, planes unable to retrieve them.

From twin rows of side-facing fabric seats, our gear piled around us, we glimpsed for nearly half an hour the vast, empty tidal mudflats of the Copper River, North America's largest West Coast wetland.

Suddenly, the plane made a looping turn and the surfline appeared through opposite windows. We were heading back to Cordova. The pilot, Pat Magie, a veteran of 15,000 flying hours, later would explain that, even with all his new electronic gadgetry, he still likes to see where he is going.

"I keep the coastline in sight," he said. "But at a certain point, it ends at some high, steep and jagged cliffs. If fog keeps me from seeing those cliffs, I turn around."

We praised his wisdom, checked into a hotel and went out for pizza.

You don't mess with Alaska. Not to catch a fish. More than any other stretch of American geography, this state exemplifies uncaring, soulless nature.

It matters not to nature whether people live or die. If we eat the bear or the bear eats us. If we hit the mountain or the tree falls or we drown in the ocean or live for another day. Nature's tedious processes just keep chipping changes over spans of thousands and millions of years.

Our goal was to reach the Tsiu River (pronounced 'sigh-you') on the Gulf of Alaska's northwestern coast. The hour's flight from picturesque Cordova, a commercial fishing village whose harbor dwarfs San Francisco's Fisherman's Wharf in charm if not in restaurants, skirts the snow-capped Chungach Mountains, immense ice fields of the Bering Glacier and the dainty foothills of Yakataga Game Refuge, Alaska's largest wintering ground for mountain goat and moose.

When we finally landed the next day on a long strip of packed sand and mud beach that separates our storm-muddied, shallow river from the pounding ocean, we encountered the newly wrecked bones of three fishing boats. They had gone down in a storm last month and recently were washed ashore. Our storm, with galelike gusts and horizontal rains that poured 18 inches overnight on Cordova, merely took a fishing tugboat and a bush plane with three lives near the town of Homer.

"Alaska has sharp elbows," I thought as we waded through waist-high waters from the landing strip to our mud-soaked tent camp in a kingdom of black fly-spawning brush between two forks of the river. "If you're not prepared to take a merciless shot or two in the ribs now and then from weather and other conditions, you have no business being here."

Thus consoled, nine of us from Chicago and Wisconsin under the leadership of Tony Portincaso embarked on a disappointing quest for silver salmon, otherwise known as large coho, as they completed their four-year life cycle in spawning runs up this normally fish-rich river.

Unfortunately, this year's run of silvers has been declared sparse by Alaska's Fish and Game Department. Bag limits abruptly were cut from three to one in many waters, including the tributaries of Cook Inlet near Anchorage. The commercial season was closed.

State biologists blamed the worst silver run in 25 years on an especially harsh winter of 1993, when streambeds froze deep and solid, killing much of that fall's salmon hatch. Four years later, this class of silvers simply was not returning in customary numbers.

A flummoxed companion who led a group from Medford, Ore., wistfully talked about the run last year.

"We came a week earlier," he said. "And fish were so thick at the mouth of the river that spinning rods caught salmon on every cast and the fly casters averaged one for every three casts. Now this was outstanding fishing."

While we experienced nothing like that, we nevertheless saw several fish in the 12-pound range. Silvers trickled into the Tsiu at high tides, chased by hungry, predatory seals. Those that escaped the seals rested in three or four holes beside broad gravel flats. While turbidity kept us from seeing them, enough fish jumped to make the heart race and keep anglers wading for hours at a time.

In three days, our little group probably hooked 150 fish, landing no more than 25 in the swift, storm-fed current. Only two came on flies, as most purists became practical and switched to egg sac-imitating Pixee spoons and straight-line spinners like Vibraxes and Mepps. The more successful anglers kept their lures on the gravelly bottom.

One fellow nearly was caught by his fish. Burly Terry Anderson of Saynor, Wis., was working a 16-pound silver toward the slippery riverbank when the current snatched his legs and toppled him onto his back.

"Lay back!" a partner yelled.

"Get rid of the rod!" screamed another.

As he was being helped to shore, we all watched forlornly as the wake of his departing tackle formed a "V" as the fish hauled it upriver. But then the "V" stopped, hung upon a gravel bar. Frank Marino of

Lincolnshire trundled out and grabbed the rod, which still held the now-exhausted fish. Anderson sloshed right after him to steer his prize safely to shore.

I spent less than half my time casting elbow to elbow with the guys for the same salmon we find in Lake Michigan. I instead waded crystal backwater pools for occasional Dolly Varden trout or perched quietly on abundant driftwood to watch eagles and trumpeter swans.

On one isolated point, I fed crumbs of crackers to half-inch trout fry swarming beside my boots, when two churring, chattering weasels emerged from the brush on either side of me.

We stood for half a minute looking into each other's eyes, the brown-coated weasels trying to figure out what I was. Never before had I been that close to these creatures in the wild.

When the sun came out and the ceiling lifted, the mountains and nearby ice fields gleamed before the lines of men and one woman relentlessly casting. Mary Ann White of Lake Forest caught a salmon on a fly, which was more than some of the unhappy others could achieve.

Salvation for a trip like this lay in ignoring the poor fishing and grasping instead the most from where we were—literally, at the edge of the earth on a treeless, flood-prone spit of sand between a storied stream and the ocean. Mountains and glaciers beamed upon us. Cries of great birds and occasional splashes of big fish cheered us. We were watched by seals and weasels.

The mess tent porch was a good place to gather in the evenings. And, of course, the Northern Lights performed at night.

February 8, 1998

Carte blanche for snow monkeys

UDANAKA, Japan—There's nothing cuter than a 2-foot-tall snow monkey diving at your feet for kernels of barley and good old Midwestern soybeans.

They skitter down the steep, rocky hillside whenever rangers at Jigokudani Yaen-koen—Japan's famous 'Hell Valley' Snow Monkey National Park—put out the feedbag three times a day.

Sometimes they become overly enthusiastic, like the monkey that followed six of us down a trail, grabbing at plastic tote bags.

It finally decided to pilfer the backpack of a fellow from Colorado Springs. His raincoat was half out before the irate monkey could be shagged away. As it left, it snatched the sack of a British woman who seemed flattered a wild monkey would want her souvenirs.

This behavior goes on throughout Japan, where an estimated 80,000 free-ranging macaques roam the nation in packs exceeding 200—in some cases rivaling America's urban deer as nuisances. Trapped when an ancestral peninsula that linked Japan to the Chinese mainland was flooded in a melting ice age, they remain the northernmost population of wild monkeys, related to macaques in Taiwan and Indonesia.

They can turn up anywhere. Grocers in town regularly fend off marauding monkeys who dash through open doorways to steal fresh produce.

Some merchants keep stinging slingshots behind their counters to teach the intruders a lesson because federal law denies them guns, and the monkeys are protected.

"It's something to see these shopkeepers pinging at the monkeys as they run down the street," said U.S. Olympic snowboarder Sondra Van Ert. "They regard them as pests– sort of like raccoons. Last year we had a bunch of the monkeys come into our hotel. They were after the fruit."

Olympic TV viewers probably will get an eyeful of these monkeys during telecasts of the snowboard competition. Macaques consider the halfpipe course part of their habitat.

"It's another group that lives up there," said Aishii Tokida, director of the monkey park. "And the ones that come into town are another group entirely."

Tokida estimates at least 10,000 macaques inhabit the Nagano Olympic region.

Because they have no predators, the monkeys thrive admirably—especially those that adapt to human handouts. Like Yellowstone bears in the days before public feedings were outlawed, they gang up for treats—and woe to the human who doesn't comply.

Just Wednesday an Italian photographer was packing his gear into a rental car when he made the mistake of leaving open a door. It turned out he also had food in that car. Six monkeys piled in, scattering his cameras and ripping out the seats and wiring. He had to call for another car.

One week earlier monkeys bit 32 people in the coastal resort of Ito. According to the Japan Times, they were mostly local folk who were attacked and nipped on the legs and ankles none apparently seriously. Although no official explanation has been issued for such unusually aggressive behavior, Tokida speculates a high monkey population density in the Ito region might make them more demanding of food.

Ito town officials have made arrangements with a local gun club to scare away the monkeys with blanks. But if that fails, shooting will be employed to thin their ranks.

Meanwhile, Olympic visitors—especially news photographers on busmen's holidays—flock to the monkey park to photograph the playful macaques. Their soulful brown eyes and thick, fluffy, silvery gray hair make them especially appealing. Baby monkeys ride past on their mothers' backs.

All the monkeys take turns soaking in special pools of hot springs water, constructed just for them. They stare benignly at clicking rows of camera lenses less than 2 feet from their faces. Often, they'll dive into outdoor public baths occupied by people at health spas.

Tokida barely suppressed a smile. Monkeys never went into these mineral baths until the park began its feeding operations in 1964, he said. Some younger ones discovered they liked the water, and the older ones followed suit.

It took a while before park personnel discovered why. The warm, relaxing water triggers bowel movements in the monkeys. As soon as park people learned this, they built pools where the water is kept at 107.6 degrees. Each night, when the monkeys go to sleep in a nearby cedar forest, park people drain the pools, scrub them out and refill them with fresh spring water.

"They look nice, and the photographers love them, but those pools really are nothing more than outhouses," Tokida said. "We use them to control the feces. Otherwise, the monkeys would do it everywhere."

Remember that the next time you're in Japan and a macaque monkey wants to share your outdoor bath.

Try to keep your composure. Offer him a magazine.

JOHN HUSAR

December 25, 1994

Christmas on the Pacific yields memorable lessons

I once spent Christmas Day in a far land, 10,000 miles from home. My friends and interests were different then. I was a scrubbed-face city youth, fresh from college, confined to an Army post on an island in the Pacific. Life yawned mysteriously before me. For all my friends, the future seemed hopefully upward, if cloudy. If only we could come home. Or find love. One or the other.

The dinner was very good that day. The Army does well for its troops on holidays. We ate all the turkey and ham and trimmings we could stuff down, then repaired to a little waterfront bar and uncapped tall bottles of sharp Japanese beer. As the sun began to set, Okinawan men in single-toed rubber boots called jikitabi filtered onto the beach. They carted mesh pots and bales of nets, and each bore an unlit lantern. Amid a spectacular sunset, they unfurled their nets, lit their lanterns and eased into the gently lapping surf. We noticed the tide was coming in.

Before long, the sky was dark and all we saw were the bobbing lights of fishermen weaving in ghostly patterns through the rocky shallows. Somehow they never tripped, never splashed blindly into a hole. They knew the water that well. Now and then they'd pull a net and put some fish into the pots. Then they would continue wading in their very sophisticated patterns.

We Americans drank our beer and quietly absorbed the ritual. The sea breeze sent us murmurs in Japanese, but mostly the men fished the inky water in silence, heads bent, searching for shadows, feeling for net tugs. The world spoke to us through those fishermen.

We could imagine coves and beaches aswarm with fishermen all around our long, narrow island, and all around the other islands throughout the China Sea. We sensed fishermen feeding their communities this Christmas night throughout the Orient, from the Korean peninsula as far south as the Philippines and the Sulus and the Malay Peninsula, even Australia, as far east as the Islands Below the Winds. The salt air that night carried a magic message.

The world to us became a community of men and women plumbing nature's largesse for the means to live another day, to raise the next generation of fishermen, of communal suppliers. Their lot in life was to learn to read the new conditions of each day, to teach children to pick their way among rocky shallows in the dead of night. Other fathers on the wind taught children to find the breadfruit in jungle trees, to sip sweet water from broad leaves, to maintain the warmth of fire in places where fuel was scarce.

Some of us in that beachfront bar went on to become physicians, nurses, salesmen, teachers, mechanics and wordsmiths, and with one or two exceptions we've never seen each other since we left that island.

But I know that here and there in America today, as on every Christmas, a scatter of once love-lost and burningly hopeful young men and women looks up from various turkey dinners and hears again the lapping of a gentle surf. They remember the dancing lantern lights on coal-black waters, and know their place in the structure of the world.

Nowadays, whenever I zoom around some gloriously abundant fishing waters, laden with technology and state-of-the-art companionship and advice, I sometimes think about those stolid men in the rubber boots who did it the old way, and I wonder if their children are out there now.

I hope their fishing waters still are good. That pollution has not wiped out the aquatic life on their reefs. That greedy long-liners and other trawling catchers of immense fish stocks have not killed their livelihoods and doomed them to the same kind of consumership so many of us now embrace-our fish arriving mainly in frozen blocks at the store.

And then I think of the trips to Chicago's lakefront for coolers of succulent perch, to Lake Erie for two days of huge walleye limits, to the year's supply of catfish that can be jugged in a single summer's night on Rend Lake.

I think of the tens of thousands of little community lakes and farm ponds that feed us our panfish whenever we bother to impale a worm. Why, we still can trek to Louisiana and come home with buckets of softshell crabs and shrimp, just for the taking.

Life can be more than good in these heady days of enlightened conservation, with more and more of us evoking a jealous interest in water quality and fish-nurturing wetlands. Hopefully, we'll stay the course and add to our numbers and strength. We need to think those lantern-bearing Okinawan fathers and uncles and brothers are out there now, maintaining a precious tradition.

I wonder where my old Army friends are, and what they got for Christmas. I'll bet most of their presents never came close to the time that Santa bore us a sense of civilization on the rise of a salty wind.

JOHN HUSAR

February 22, 1988

He sees the Olympic sights, doesn't miss skating beat

CALGARY–As speedskaters well know, the 10,000-meter race is inescapable.

Even when you try.

The thing goes on and on and on.

I tried to do my duty Sunday and spend the day at the Olympic Oval, where 32 skaters were destined to take their turns at this icy marathon that eventually would be won by Sweden's Tomas Gustafson, his second gold of the Games.

But this is no ordinary marathon, where the athletes hurry off to see who finishes first.

This one is done on a pair of lanes, slowly and methodically, two skaters at a time, strictly against the clock.

Each pair skates 25 laps, or 6.2 miles, lasting about 15 minutes. After three pairs, there's a 25-minute break while the ice is resurfaced. Then three more pairs. Then another resurface.

And so on.

It was 12:02 when the first skater responded to the gun, and I was there, pen poised for the drama.

By six laps, the blue-clad mustachioed Soviet was half a lap ahead of the gray-clad West German.

The big moment came in the 22nd lap, when the Soviet lapped his struggling opponent.

At 12:18, the first heat had ended and 15 more remained. It was time to get some air. I got in the car and drove across town to Canada Olympic Park to see how the bobsledders were doing. Traffic was light, but the heavy winds were blowing sand from the snowless countryside across the track, and the race was postponed just as I reached the top of the hill.

It was nice, though, to sit and watch the countryside, the sprawl of Calgary through the Canadian Rocky foothills. I tooled around some back roads and found Broadcast Hill, the housing village for the electronic media, and drove inside to peek at the TV monitors.

The third pair still was on the ice. The big news was that some fellow had fallen, gotten up, recovered his lost five seconds and still beat the other guy in his heat. I had a slice of pizza and drove on.

Back at the Oval, they were resurfacing, so I took a walk across the splendid University of Calgary campus to the Nickel Art Museum and spent some time among the special displays of Olympic coins and athletic art.

The centerpieces were turn-of-the-century bronzes by Canadian sculptor Robert Tait McKenzie that mainly featured naked Greeks with boxing gloves and figure skates, which made me wonder how those Greeks made ice on Mt. Olympus. I checked, and the fourth pair was on the ice.

The commuter rail station was a couple of blocks away, so I caught a train to Stampede Park, nine stops, where I stepped into the Corral Arena just in time to see the top U.S. ice dancing team waltz through their third compulsory dance before a house full of mostly empty seats. Unfortunately, Suzanne Semanick chose that moment to tumble daintily on her derriere, but that didn't seem to faze the judges, for the scores were decent. Semanick and her partner, Scott Gregory, wound up fifth.

I sat next to a gray-haired gentleman named Bob Bishopp, who drove 900 miles from Powell, Wyo., to take in the Games with his wife. He said he didn't understand figure skating judges, either.

"I mean, I've seen some performances by kids that were just superb,but they didn't get any scores," Bishopp said. "I guess it's good I'm not a judge. I guess I just don't know when they're sticking their toes in the ice right or not."

By then, it was 2:30 and I ambled across the fairgrounds to the Saddledome to drop in on the Soviet-Czech hockey game. The second period was just beginning, and I turned my head just in time to see Soviet star Vladimir Krutov score the first of his two goals to make the score 3-0.

I tried to find a seat in press row, but all were taken. As I ducked up and down the aisle, a couple of young Canadians working in the statistics department took pity and let me squeeze into a chair between them in the aisle at the top of the rows of seats.

"Mr. Tretiak is sitting behind us," whispered Kevin Umscheid of Milo, Alberta, indicating a shadow in the luxury box above. I asked if the great ex-Soviet goalie was hawking his book, and Kevin answered, very seriously, that he "didn't see any copies of his book."

We giggled at the specter of Czech and Soviet skaters milling around the ice during a timeout to the organ strains of "Lucky, Lucky, Lucky Me; I'm a Lucky Sonovagun." Kevin pointed out No. 24 on the

Czechs, Jiri Hrdina, who has signed to play with the Calgary Flames after the Games.

"He's already bought a house in town," Kevin reported.

About that time, Krutov scored his second goal and it was 4-0 Soviets, so I decided to be on my way.

I stopped for some ice cream rolled in chocolate and peanuts, wandered into the main press center and checked again with the Oval.

This time, the voice in on the phone was excited. "There's a fellow on the ice who's breaking a record," exclaimed press room aide Theresa Goulet.

I checked a TV monitor and, indeed, Sweden's Gustafson, skating in the ninth pair, was about to plummet across the finish line in a world-record 13 minutes 48.20 seconds.

I watched him pant into a microphone about how he stuck to his own schedule and tried not to be distracted by the crowd and about how happy he was to win another medal, including the 5,000 meters.

I checked my start list and saw that Americans Eric Flaim and Jeff Klaiber were to skate next, but the ice was being resurfaced again and it would be a while.

I cashed some traveler's checks, made a few more phone calls and chatted with some friends. Then Flaim and Klaiber were on the ice. The monitor showed they had little chance for a medal. Although Flaim did come in fourth for the third time in these Games, he was more than five seconds behind bronze-winning Leo Visser of the Netherlands. It was 4 p.m., and still there were six pairs to go.

I caught a train to the Olympic Plaza downtown, where thousands already were gathering for the evening's medal ceremonies. Crews were practicing the anthems, and the air was heavy with hot dogs and mustard.

I peered into the huge Coca-Cola Food Fair tent, where a chorus of Scottish ladies in tartans was performing on the stage and the line outside stretched a block to get in.

For two weeks, I'd wanted to watch the pin-traders hustle, but I always was too busy. Now, during the 10,000-meter race, I finally had the time. Back on the train, mobbed now with hockey fans, I finally found a seat and took a nap.

The air was cool and bracing as I walked across the campus as twilight fell. I stopped first at the Student Union and gave Theresa another call. Three more pairs were still to skate.

That was nice, because I was hungry and I knew of a nice little Korean food stand where I could get a plate of spicy pork with vegetables and dumplings.

That was so good, I indulged in a double espresso and a chocolate-banana bran muffin for dessert. I read one of the Sunday papers.

I suspected that I really should get back to work. I quickly hiked the two blocks to the Oval, alarmed that perhaps I was a little late. People were streaming from the arena. I hurried through the door and, for once, no one was there to check my credential. I bounded up the stairs and, lo, before a crowd now of only a few hundred, some guys were still out there skating.

I sat down and watched the final pair.

Nothing had happened. Nothing had changed.

Gustafson still was the leader, and Flaim still was in fourth.

A couple of other journalists looked at me with weary eyes. They wanted to know where I'd been.

"Around," I said, reaching for a cup of coffee. "I guess you could say I've been here all the time."

CHAPTER TEN
LIVING WILL

John Husar's ultimate gift to readers was sharing his feelings about life and death in the decidedly public forum of a big-city newspaper. We are too often hesitant in today's world to lay out our fears or longings, even privately to our loved ones. We avoid saying what's on our minds or what resides in our hearts because we don't want to look vulnerable or hurt someone's feelings.

Most of all, we clutch on talking about death. John did just the opposite. He explained to readers what was happening to his body during illness. We were privy to some of his most intimate thoughts, as evidenced in this chapter.

Rather than pity himself or invite readers to sympathize, John quietly became more personal in his writings. He urged us to sit still once in a while, appreciate a sunny meadow or the porch swing. He wrote about loyal dogs and old friends. He wrote about sunsets, without calling attention to his own.

John lived a full and strong-willed life. Anyone who has read a story of his knows that. And we are all a little better equipped for life because of it.

February 3, 1999

Walter, we're in this together

About the only words of comfort I can offer Walter Payton are, wel-come to the club.

You have joined about 12,000 of us in America who are waiting for a liver transplant.

The fact that only half of us will get one this year is the shaky part. The donor rate isn't as good as it should be in this age of enlighten-ment. A lot of otherwise generous people remain queasy about organ donations. Perhaps you—and, to a smaller extent, columns such as this can create a better awareness.

My problem is a little different from yours. I have Hepatitis C, the latest boutique disease. Doctors have just begun to track its raging path through the populace. They fear this new epidemic may kill more Americans than AIDS.

Unlike the more common and controllable Hepatitises A and B, "Hep C" lurks for years after a viral infection. Its main avenue of trans-mission is through infected blood. That's why a lot of its victims are drug users who share dirty needles. Another bunch is unfortunate medical workers who intimately contact the blood of others.

That's how I figure I got this disease. I was a medic in the Army Reserve, a surgical technician and emergency room attendant who often had bloody hands. We didn't worry much then about blood-borne disease. No one really thought of it. If you were stuck by some-one's suture needle or nicked by a used scalpel, all you did was change gloves and go on. Now we know better. But for some, it's too late.

My disease cooked quietly for years until a rash of inexplicable blood poisonings weakened my immune system enough to trigger fully flowering Hep C. A pair of wonderful doctors diagnosed me in 1992, only three years after the disease had been given a name. Until then it was known only as "non-A, non-B hepatitis," which seemed to me an awful lot of latitude.

But either way—my Hepatitis C or your primary sclerosing cholangitis—the liver weakens and dies. Hopefully, we'll get new ones in plenty of time to live full and reasonably normal lives.

But now there is that other factor—the one that truly gives me chills. The worst part of waiting for a liver donation that may save my life is knowing someone else has to die.

I realize this death will not be my fault. I will not have ordered the car wreck, gunshot or fatal plunge to brain death that leaves a victim hopeless of recovery. I will not sit in a hospital antechamber with the grieving family and friends who have been asked to make an awesome decision. I know this is simply a statistical matter of numbers.

I will go about my business in blissful ignorance, hoping for some anonymous match, anticipating a call night or day. Will the bleeping wail of my medical beeper interrupt some deer hunt, birthday party or afternoon of fishing? Is an accident happening now that will change the course of my life as well as the lives of another family?

I feel myself careering along a frightful path as two of us race toward a fateful intersection.

Which leads to the next step. If I am to benefit from the loss of another's life, I owe that person a responsibility not to waste this precious gift. I owe that victim—and his or her family—a meaningful contribution. The two of us must mesh to make this a bit of a better world.

If I can't hold up that end of the bargain, I don't believe I should deserve another's liver.

I'll admit this whole process leaves me a little scared. This is no simple procedure. There are no guarantees of survival, although the odds are good. Most get past these surgeries well enough to worry about rejection. Powerful drugs offset rejection by inhibiting the immune system. You basically fool it into failing to recognize the new liver as a foreign intruder. But that leaves you wide open to any other kind of infection, and that's where a lot of problems lie.

Personally, I choose not to worry. Worrying never changed a thing. It never caught a fish or won a football game. It never caught a bride or made a grandson proud.

Worrying basically gets in the way of important things like being needled by your friends, having them order fried liver when you go out, having them ask you to pick out a handsome, healthy guy whom they can kidnap to the medical center. If I can't use the liver, they figure maybe I can get the face.

Constant worry just makes others uneasy and afraid to say what's on their minds, afraid to ask what needs to be asked.

Worrying is a great way to leave yourself isolated and lonely.

I choose instead to treat this as an adventure. Not quite as scintillating as a trip to the North Pole or an Amazonian jungle, but at least as good a roller-coaster ride as any at Great America.

Since joining the transplant list last October I am seeing some wonderful things and meeting some of the nicest, most heroic and supportive people I'll ever know. I am feeling the power of prayer.

By remaining upbeat and in high spirits, I know I'll make this easier on the loved ones around me.

And as for my fine doctors and excellent transplant team at Rush Medical Center? Well, we'll try to keep each other in stitches, one way or another, until it's time to go home.

February 9, 2000

Lives sadly end, but wait and hope don't

And so it came down to the ugly reality that Walter Payton could not be helped with a liver transplant at all.

He was caught too far in the claws of cancer for any organ donation to make a difference.

This, of course, is no comfort to the 66,513 people who await transplants of some type in America. That includes the 14,092 of us on the liver waiting list who—like Payton did for a tragically short while—are betting our lives upon the generosity of strangers.

Likewise, there is only sadness for the untold volume of men and women who responded to Payton's tearful, televised plight eight months ago by nobly declaring their desire to become organ donors.

People seemed to believe that, by being willing to share the gift of life, they in some way could help Walter.

Under different circumstances, any increased flow of donor organs might have done just that. More organs would mean earlier transplants for many of us who face the terrible fear that we might die before a suitable organ becomes available.

Organs, you see, just don't pop up like treats in a vending machine. Just because you need one doesn't mean you'll get one.

Only 4,479 people received liver transplants last year, which is less than a third of the demand. In 1998, no less than 1,327 people died because they couldn't get a suitably matched liver in time.

For those of us on the waiting list, the most important question at the Payton family press conference was not answered. That was whether Payton could have survived had his debilitating liver disease been diagnosed before the cancer had spread and a transplant no longer was feasible.

The answer probably is yes. Payton would have zoomed upward on the scale of critical need. A healthy liver would have been found for him and he would be with us today, making those squeaky-voiced bantering phone calls to his pals across the land.

But despite Payton's awesome talents and the incredible esteem and love he earned, he just wasn't lucky enough. Fate does not respect celebrity.

Walter's illness did give heart to numerous transplant candidates who believed the attention he drew might step up the flow of donor organs. He more than anyone else made multitudes of people aware of the goodness that can come from sharing loved ones' organs.

All of us in the boat became connected to him. People would ask us for the inside dope on Walter, as if we somehow could penetrate his intense privacy.

We would say what we hoped others might say about us, that we didn't know a thing about Walter's condition, but we certainly hoped he would get his liver in time.

Of course, we didn't know about the cancer.

There was an ominous sign when the word leaked three or four weeks ago that Payton had not received a medical beeper to summon him to surgery upon a moment's notice. Surely by now he would have been issued a beeper, considering his clear decline and fatigue. I've had mine for a year. If Walter didn't have a beeper, something else— something bad—had to be going on.

Why, Walter hadn't even played "backup," which happens to suitable candidates whenever a transplant is scheduled. One or two backups always are summoned to be on hand just in case something goes wrong with the primary designee.

Most of the time it's a long shot, but you never know. Given the paucity of donor organs, doctors cannot risk wasting a good one that cannot be sewn into the primary recipient for any reason such as size or a sudden illness.

I have gotten to play "backup" three times at Rush Medical Center. Once there was a question of whether a woman could accept a larger liver. I was bigger, so I was invited to wait and see.

But since she had to have this liver or die, the prayers of my family were with her. We all were glad when we left the hospital and caught a glimpse of her family at peaceful rest in the surgical waiting room.

The second time we knew the fellow at the end of the hall would have no problems, so I never even changed my clothes. My wife gave his wife a big hug of hope as he was wheeled to the operating room.

Not too long ago I was back at Rush again, this time prepped fully with IVs and antibiotics because another patient might be too unstable to survive the ordeal of surgery. But our good doctors spent hours to elevate her strength sufficiently, and she seems to be doing well.

So we march on, waiting and hoping. All of us continue to wait and hope.

Only now we won't have Payton as our brother in need, and the strength and joy we knew he would give us by pulling through.

JOHN HUSAR

February 9, 2000

It's great to be out of the woods, and in the woods

A weird thing happened on my way into the country to check on a Christmas tree.

At one point I gazed appreciatively upon a sere, wintry Illinois landscape rolling beyond the car's windows. The next I was flat on my back for three days, unable to slip outside the cabin for even a moment to sniff a breath of fresh air.

Then came a gloomy procession through hospitals, six days in one, 10 in another. There were morbid tests with bad results. Friends gathered, many on their knees.

One day my pastor, Jack Wall of Old St. Pat's, had the audacity to ask for a miracle and darned if he didn't get one. Several fine doctors at one of Chicago's great medical centers still thumb through my stack of scans and tests, wondering how they guessed so wrong.

They hadn't guessed wrong; they simply were overruled.

It took a month and a half before I lurched back into the woods. I knew I was healed of this sudden infection then, although my major quest for a new liver remains at bay. Until then I can resume going where I have to be.

We all need different reassurances. Some of us just cannot feel alive until we hunker upon a bucket, dipping minnows or grubs through frosty holes in the ice.

Others need a ride on a powerful snow sled along empty trails bordered by wilderness. Most gladly will settle for a hickory log fire in a little cabin in the woods.

I'll buy that, of course, but I also need to walk in those woods. To prowl game trails at my own languid pace, gathering clues to lives that mostly are mysteries to our kind of cumbersome two-legged mammals.

It is those four-legged creatures who teach us the deepest truths of the woods.

Follow a deer path a mile or so and you'll learn of 20 different ways to hide from inclement weather.

Pause at intersections with fox trails, squirrel trails, raccoon trails, even the dainty, lacy pathways of field mice.

Take time to study those smaller game trails and you'll learn the danger points, where prancing paws brake to watch and ponder.

In softer ground, you easily can tell which way a critter leaned, when he turned, when he made his next decision. You can just about imagine what he saw.

One of my prouder tracking moments occurred under the tutelage of a master named Tom Hanratty. I'd lain upon the ground to survey an estab-

lished rabbit run with the idea of setting a snare, when I noticed the stalk-
ing footprints of a fox.

Then way down on the floor of this faint disturbance of wild grass, I saw
an old, tiny zigzag pathway made by the routine passage of rodents.

This turned out to be their trail, their route from seed supply to burrow.
It was this signal that the rabbit noticed and the fox behind him and, eventually—always seeking the path of least resistance—that most practical of
woodland creatures, the savvy deer.

I knew then I was a tracker, that I could read the woods as well as my
angling guru Spence Petros can read the waters and recognize conditions
hidden beneath the waves. He has tried to impart to me that special talent
with little success for 15 years.

Imagine tracking the water's surface. Impossible. To dolts like me, anyway.

Those of us who track only what they see are best served by a fresh,
new snowfall. We've had a few of those in recent weeks—soft, clean blankets covering the trashy disturbances out there, including horse-like
human steps, sandwich wrappers and gouges from wind-blown tree limbs.

A new snow is a fresh canvas for nature's exquisite art, for patterns of
footsteps that reveal keys to life in these harshest of months, but months
of abundance for many animals.

You can sit on a log and notice dribbles of plant seeds beside spun patterns of mousy steps. Look close enough and you'll locate gateways to
secret hideaways and snug dens where winter is only a suggestion.

Deer steps idle past, revealing favored routes between food and shelter
as well as the sizes and numbers of the herd.

The raccoons, pesky creatures of habit, already will have Zambonied an
unswerving icy path from den tree to forage area.

With luck, you'll see the track and scat of fox or coyote, always on a
major path, always where the view is far and beneficial.

In better times, I'd stay out for hours, mostly in the wan light of dawn or
dusk when movements are likely and you see nearly as much as you hear.
But now I'm more than partial to that hickory fire and the smoke-wafted
memories of physically stronger days.

There'll be a few more rocky moments ahead, I know, but you can't
imagine, you just can't, what it meant to me to come back at last into my
proper place in those woods.